Transpoetic Exchange

Bucknell Studies in Latin American Literature and Theory

Series editor: Aníbal González, Yale University

Dealing with far-reaching questions of history and modernity, language and selfhood, and power and ethics, Latin American literature sheds light on the many-faceted nature of Latin American life, as well as on the human condition as a whole. This highly successful series has published some of the best recent criticism on Latin American literature. Acknowledging the historical links and cultural affinities between Latin American and Iberian literatures, the series productively combines scholarship with theory and welcomes consideration of Spanish and Portuguese texts and topics, while also providing a space of convergence for scholars working in Romance studies, comparative literature, cultural studies, and literary theory.

Selected Titles in the Series

Rebecca E. Biron, *Elena Garro and Mexico's Modern Dreams*
Persephone Brahman, *From Amazons to Zombies: Monsters in Latin America*
Jason Cortés, *Macho Ethics: Masculinity and Self-Representation in Latino-Caribbean Narrative*
Tara Daly, *Beyond Human: Vital Materialisms in the Andean Avant-Gardes*
Earl E. Fitz, *Machado de Assis and Female Characterization: The Novels*
Earl E. Fitz, *Machado de Assis and Narrative Theory: Language, Imitation, Art, and Verisimilitude in the Last Six Novels*
Naida García-Crespo, *Early Puerto Rican Cinema and Nation Building: National Sentiments, Transnational Realities, 1897–1940*
Thomas S. Harrington, *Public Intellectuals and Nation Building in the Iberian Peninsula, 1900–1925: The Alchemy of Identity*
David Kelman, *Counterfeit Politics: Secret Plots and Conspiracy Narratives in the Americas*
Brendan Lanctot, *Beyond Civilization and Barbarism: Culture and Politics in Postrevolutionary Argentina*
Marília Librandi, Jamille Pinheiro Dias, and Tom Winterbottom, eds., *Transpoetic Exchange: Haroldo de Campos, Octavio Paz, and Other Multiversal Dialogues*
Adriana Méndez Rodenas, *Transatlantic Travels in Nineteenth-Century Latin America: European Women Pilgrims*
Andrew R. Reynolds, *The Spanish American Crónica Modernista, Temporality, and Material Culture*
Elisa Sampson Vera Tudela, *Ricardo Palma's Tradiciones: Illuminating Gender and Nation*
Mary Beth Tierney-Tello, *Mining Memory: Reimagining Self and Nation through Narratives of Childhood in Peru*

Transpoetic Exchange

Haroldo de Campos, Octavio Paz, and Other Multiversal Dialogues

EDITED BY MARÍLIA LIBRANDI, JAMILLE PINHEIRO DIAS, AND TOM WINTERBOTTOM

Bucknell University | University Press
Lewisburg, Pennsylvania

Library of Congress Cataloging-in-Publication Data

Names: Rocha, Marília Librandi, editor. | Pinheiro Dias, Jamille, editor. | Winterbottom, Tom, editor.
Title: Transpoetic exchange : Haroldo de Campos, Octavio Paz, and other multiversal dialogues / edited by Marília Librandi, Jamille Pinheiro Dias, Tom Winterbottom.
Description: Lewisburg, Pennsylvania : Bucknell University Press, 2020. | Series: Bucknell studies in Latin American literature and theory | Includes bibliographical references and index.
Identifiers: LCCN 2019035843 | ISBN 9781684482177 (hardback) | ISBN 9781684482160 (paperback) | ISBN 9781684482184 (epub)
Subjects: LCSH: Campos, Haroldo de—Criticism and interpretation. | Paz, Octavio, 1914–1998—Criticism and interpretation. | Poetry—Translating.
Classification: LCC PQ9697.C2448 Z877 2020 | DDC 861/.62—dc23
LC record available at https://lccn.loc.gov/2019035843

A British Cataloging-in-Publication record for this book is available from the British Library.

∞ The paper used in this publication meets the requirements of the American National Standard for Information Sciences—Permanence of Paper for Printed Library Materials, ANSI Z39.48-1992.

www.bucknell.edu/UniversityPress

Distributed worldwide by Rutgers University Press

Manufactured in the United States of America

Uma arte—não q apresente—mas q presentifique
—"Olho por olho a nu (Manifesto)," Haroldo de Campos

Contents

Transpoetic Exchange

Introduction

A Multiversal Experiment

MARÍLIA LIBRANDI, JAMILLE PINHEIRO DIAS, AND TOM WINTERBOTTOM

Octavio Paz (1914–1998) wrote "Blanco" (1966) while serving as the Mexican ambassador to India. It is a poem of audacious scope, a venture that dialogues with Stéphane Mallarmé's "Un Coup de Dès" (1898) and the eighth-century A.D. Hevajra Tantra, an Indo-Tibetan Tantric Buddhist philosophy based on the mandala's meditation to attain *sunyata*. In the resulting work, Paz creates an eroticized poem that points to a supreme state of being in nothingness or of being present while disappearing, much like light emanating from dying stars or the reverberation of silence.

Blanco. The word already creates a sense of intrigue. In English, it translates as three things: white, blank, and target. The poem is a Mexican and Spanish American take on two distinct Eastern and Western traditions: a Latin American incorporation of French Symbolist poetry and the philosophy of Tantric Buddhism. That was not the end of it, however. With the publication of *Transblanco* (1986), the Brazilian poet Haroldo de Campos (1929–2003)—himself a central figure of world literature from Latin America, an innovative twentieth-century Brazilian poet—produced a volume that incorporated a translation of Paz's work as well as correspondence between Paz and Campos from 1968 to 1981 and essays by literary critics and writers such as Julio Ortega and Paulo Leminski. Since its publication, *Transblanco* has become a model of what poetic pluri-dialogues can achieve through translation understood as "transcreation," as Haroldo de Campos called it.

The link between Paz and Campos goes beyond just this particular (and important) translation, and it extends to a sustained friendship and ongoing intellectual exchange. In editing the present book, we take Paz and Campos's friendship to foreground the relational aspects of poetry and translation, and so we have brought together an international network of contemporary literary critics, poets, and visual artists who have been influenced or impacted by their intellectual and personal relationship. The choice of prefix—"trans-"—in Campos's book title has a double function: first, it refers to transversal cultural interactions and existences; and second (albeit inexorably linked to the first), it refers to the transformations that take place in the course of these relationships and processes. The "trans-" aspect is often sidelined when it comes to discussions of originality and authorship, when in fact the case of Paz and Campos exemplifies this type of exchange that operates trans-linguistically, trans-culturally, and trans-continentally.

The works that inspired this project include not only "Blanco" and *Transblanco* but also Campos's *Galáxias*, which he began in 1963 and finished in 1976. This work again conveys an instance of this artistic exchange: it is a collection that defies conventional categories of prose and poetry. In Campos's words, this "kaleidoscopic book" is an "audiovideotext, videotextogram," uniting "narrative gestures" with epiphanic moments, written to be read aloud with words "carrying a mantric, 'transmental' value."[1] Those prerogatives have a clear resonance with Paz's intentions.

At least three related aspects unite Paz and Campos as poet-thinkers beyond the specific personal and creative textual correspondences. In the first place, poetry is at the core of their action and their worlds, and they consider everything—existence, transcendence, language—under the gaze of and in the light of poetry. In the second place, they integrate the world tradition of poetic self-reflection through the image of light and mutual illuminations (oftentimes expressed as blanks and the white spaces on a page), as is the case in "Blanco" and *Transblanco*. Finally, both poets signal the direction of poetry as that of translation, which is understood as the embodiment of otherness and of a poetic tradition that every new poem brings back again as a Babel re-enacted. These intellectual and artistic affinities, as manifested particularly in "Blanco," *Transblanco*, and *Galáxias*, were the main axes around which we organized an international colloquium and poetic performance at Stanford University in January 2010. This volume is a print corollary to and expansion of that event.

The present volume brings together scholars and artists to rethink and discuss Paz and Campos's poetic friendship as centered on the aforementioned triad of books from a perspective that privileges transcultural dialogues. The texts serve as a point of departure, rather than arrival, in a quest to produce contemporary movements in thinking and poetics that move in various directions and as inspired by the spirit of the various writers, critics, and artists brought together here. In this sense, comparisons were made to amplify these three "source" texts (even though they themselves, of course, have multiple sources) in time and in space to bring them into focus again in the twenty-first century. We have brought together essays of an academic as well as personal nature, as well as artistic expressions that follow the works' intense and condensed capacity to produce an immediate synthesis of the multiple in their essence and motivation. Though we take the specific case of Paz and Campos and their interactions as the central topic, part of our aim is to promote conversations at large around the idea of poetry and translation as a relational and interactive site.

We have divided the present volume into three parts. The first part, "Essays," unites seven texts by scholars who focus on the relationship between the two authors and the three texts, their antecedents, their impact and influence, and their cultural resonance. The second part, "Remembrances," focuses on the images reflected in the remembrance of intellectual interactions with Campos. The third part, "Poems," includes poems by contemporary authors from Brazil, Japan, and the United States who share their art as creations inspired in large measure by the influence and impact of Paz and Campos.

According to Alfred Gell, "ambassadors are real persons"; however, "they are also 'fictions.'"[2] A Chinese ambassador, for example, "does not look like China, but in London, China looks like him."[3] Paz's political and cultural posting in India was profoundly important for his work as a poet, and it was here that his "fictional" existence as an ambassador brought into clear relief the transcontinental and transcultural aspects of his creative being. He was appointed ambassador to India in 1962, and he held this position until 1968, when he resigned from the Mexican foreign service in protest against the massacre of Tlatelolco. It was during this time that he would write "Blanco," a title on which he later expanded: "*Blanco*: white; blank; an unmarked space, emptiness; the white mark in the center of a target."[4]

For Campos to take on his transcreation of "Blanco" was not an unexpected surprise but rather the marking of an intellectual resonance that was part of a broader Latin American literary and cultural debate. Campos, for his part, had been working at the same time on his own supernova in the form of *Galáxias*, the stellar explosion of light and nothingness represented by words and space on the page. As a central figure in Brazilian concretist poetry and the founder of the Noigandres group and magazine, Campos enjoyed an open creative dialogue with Paz, and this would later find itself transformed into actual correspondence. With Campos's *Transblanco*, however, we have an example not only of a Brazilian-Mexican dialogue but of a broader concern: the volume's preface is signed by the Uruguayan literary critic Emir Rodríguez Monegal, who, at that time, was professor at the Department of Spanish and Portuguese at Yale University. The section "Em torno a Blanco" includes essays by other literary critics, among them the Peruvian Julio Ortega, who was professor at the University of Texas, Austin, where both Paz (1969) and Campos (1981) had visited for scholarly positions and intellectual missions. It was during Campos's time in Texas as a visiting scholar that he decided to translate "Blanco." *Transblanco* is, then, not only the result of a Latin American poetic partnership but one that was reinforced in the United States, adding an Anglo-American component to this Luso-Hispanic configuration that could be claimed as a model for a comparatist work that stretches beyond the papal line of Tordesillas/Tordesilhas and into a trans-American realm.

To borrow the title of Kirsten Silva Gruesz's book on nineteenth-century U.S. Latino writers, we argue that Paz and Campos acted as twentieth-century Latin American "ambassadors of culture."[5] Their work, and specifically these comings-together, has poetry and poetics at its heart, and these serve as the foundation for their political, historical, and sociological thought. When Campos identifies translation as the pathway for what he understands as post-utopian poetry, he is referring not only to the translation of a poem from one language to another (which in itself is significant) but to translation as the source of the poem's (re)creation, its "transcreation." It is an invention that is intrinsically invaded by voices other than the author's, an effect that is achieved by evoking or alluding to an external and foreign tradition, a vision that is similar to what Paz proposes in *La otra voz* (1990).[6] In that vision, the images of light, transparency, space, blankness, and mutual illuminations play a fundamental role in the expression on the page, and it is with this in mind that we turn to the edition in hand.

The first contribution to the "Essays" section comes from Enrico Mario Santí, who offers an exploration of the "presence of absence" in "Blanco." João Adolfo Hansen then analyzes the modern and post-utopic at work between "Blanco" and *Transblanco*, before Marjorie Perloff examines the impact of Ezra Pound's translation techniques on Paz and Campos, incorporating the latter's *Galáxias* in her analysis. Marília Librandi then considers the transparency, blankness, and white space of Paz's and Campos's poetry as the image (or absence of image) that both use in their defense of poetry. After this, Antonio Cicero traces the presence of the "modern" and the "avant-garde" in "post-utopian" poetry, after which Luiz Costa Lima examines what "Blanco" derived from the impact and reach of Stéphane Mallarmé, and particularly his "Un coup de dés." In the final essay, Odile Cisneros examines the poetics and translational practices of the Noigandres group and Octavio Paz and their interactions.

The second section, "Remembrances," collects three experiences of interaction with Campos in the process of transcreating "Blanco" and working on *Transblanco* and *Galáxias*. Charles A. Perrone remembers the fruitful academic connection that Campos maintained with his "Austineia Desvairada" after the latter's first visit as a visiting professor in 1971 and his 1981 return, when Perrone met him. Next, Kenneth David Jackson remembers his extended relationship with Campos—from thesis advice in São Paulo to the invitation to Austin—and the creative impulse that Campos drew from his time in Texas. Finally, Benedito Nunes recollects his meeting with Campos at the University of Texas in 1981, recalling the proximity between poetry and philosophy for which Campos argued. In the third section, "Poems," poets of international standing and renown—Charles Bernstein, Antonio Cicero, Jerome Rothenberg, Keijiro Suga, and André Vallias—share their creations.

Between these two artists, and this conjunction of scholars and artists, we have "Campos de Paz": fields of peace that are nourished by multiversal dialogue. In addition to relaying intimate and creative reflections on the authors' works, the present collection contributes to and expands on existing scholarship on the subject. Ignacio Infante's 2013 book *After Translation: The Transfer and Circulation of Modern Poetics across the Atlantic* provides an important foundation for our study for its focus on the "ways in which the circulation of modern poetry and poetics is articulated by the translation of various poetic traditions and forms across the diverse spatiotemporal realm of meditation constituted by the Atlantic Ocean," and we add Paz and Campos to this important intuition while also expanding its reach to other realms and channels across the Americas and beyond.[7] The wide-ranging 2014 collection edited by Roberto Cantú, *The Willow and the Spiral: Essays on Octavio Paz and the Poetic Imagination*, provides vital perspectives on Paz and the internationality of his poetic reach, while not addressing "Blanco" in detail; to this we also add a comparative dimension by incorporating Campos.[8] In putting together this collection, we are also indebted to the essays collected by Lisa Block de Behar (2009) and the collection organized by Leda Tenório da Motta (2005), both on Haroldo de Campos.[9] Several other articles on "Blanco" inspired our perspectives on Paz's work, including those by Victoria Carpenter, Juan Malpartida, and Clara Román-Odio.[10] Additionally, Rodolfo Mata Sandoval has important articles, interviews, and translations that bring together Paz and Campos in dialogue, providing an intellectual backdrop that nourished the present volume, as does the aptly titled article "América Latina Reinventada," by Maria Esther Maciel.[11]

With these inspirations and references in mind, our proposal is not only to interpret but also to relate; it is to see how these texts move us and how we can move them to understand their intense and condensed capacity to produce an immediate synthesis of the multiple. Our aim is to experiment with these texts and their origins to see how they inspire engagement and reflection that is itself a journey across multiple worlds in how the authors here collected have chosen to understand and relate the impact of the spirit of transcreation on their own creative beings. In this spirit, we have welcomed and encouraged comparisons that amplify Campos's and Paz's work vertically in time or horizontally in space, or a combination of the two. This textual encounter between Paz and Campos allows us to propose another multiversal poetic experiment, a parallel chant in homage to "Blanco" and *Transblanco*: a trans-linguistic, transcultural, and trans-continental way to work through comparisons with compassion and a shared passion that promises to produce differences and to multiply singularities through (un)expected and desired encounters. It is in this spirit that we invite you to enjoy this volume.

Part I

Essays

1

On the Presence of Absence

Octavio Paz's "Blanco"

ENRICO MARIO SANTÍ

If I had to summarize the sensation I experienced completing editorial work on Octavio Paz's *Blanco/Archivo Blanco* it would be my title: the paradox of the presence of absence. At the end of "Esto no es un poema" (This is not a poem), my 1996 essay, I reflected on how the concluding lines "La irrealidad de lo mirado / da realidad a la mirada" (The unreality of the seen / gives reality to the seeing) describe not only the vanishing bodies of the two lovers whose erotic experience the poem describes but also the vanishing of the text itself.[1] My point was not that the end of the poem allegorizes its own narrative ending—a trite theme and procedure in modernist art; instead, I wanted to show that the poem's running argument against all forms of relativism reaches one devastating conclusion: all matter, including all bodies, and including the text we are reading, dissolves as soon as we reach a stage of silence after the word.

"Silence after the word," precisely the poem's target (which *blanco* also means in Spanish), could therefore be reduced neither to a mystical experience nor to a vulgar nihilism. In the poem's context, and indeed the poet's, it refers to Buddhist relative silence, *sunyata*, as defined in Madhyamaka, the Buddhist school of Nagarjuna. An explanation of this concept appears in Paz's book on Lévi-Strauss, the contents of which date from 1966, the same year he published

Blanco. "There are two silences," he wrote, "one before the word, a desire to say; another, after the word, the knowledge that the only thing worth saying cannot be said."[2] In yet another text from the same year he added: "The poem is the trajectory between these two silences—between the wish to speak and the silence that fuses the wishing and the speaking."[3] Obviously, these reflections point not only to the distinction between two types of silence: before and after the word, before and after the experience of poetry; they also attempt to get at the meaning of meaning. "The Buddha's silence," he also wrote, "neither affirms nor denies. It says something else, and it alludes to a beyond which is right here. It says: *Sunyata*: everything is empty because everything is full, the word is not a saying because the only saying is silence. Not nihilism but a relativism that destroys and goes beyond itself."[4] Indeed, a summary of this idea appears in those final lines of "Blanco": "The unreality of the seen / gives reality to the seeing." "Lo mirado," the seen, according to a comment that Paz made to an early draft of my own essay, which I cited then and re-cite now, "is the world of relative relations. As soon as we discover it, relativism opens up and lets us see the other side: untouchable and unsayable reality, a vision that also gives reality to us, mortal creatures, mere accidents in the chain of evolution."[5]

Thus, at the end of "Blanco," the paradox of an absence of presence takes hold by virtue of one fact: by then the reader has gone through an extremely elaborate *material* experience; radical presence yields to radical absence. Such material experience takes place on at least three levels. First, it becomes literally palpable with actual physical production: the reader must unfold all thirty-two sheets, the text's 552 centimeters—a physical, sometimes awkward activity that harks back to precursor texts like Blaise Cendrars and Sonia Delaunay's *Prose du Transibérien* (1913), not to mention Mallarmé's "Un coup de dés" (written in 1897). In the case of "Blanco" the experience is related to Buddhism and, specifically, as we shall see, to Tantric ritual.

In 1969, when "Blanco" was included in *Ladera este/Eastern Slope*, the poems Paz wrote earlier in the decade in India, the poem's unfolding was lost with its reprint in book format. Paz did use the occasion, however, to point out that the poem "ought to be read" as "a succession of signs on a single page; as the reading progresses, the page unfolds: a space that in its movement allows the text to appear and that, in a way, produces it."[6] It became clear that text production was very much linked, in Paz's mind, to unfolding the poem's single sheet. It was also clear that this central feature would be lost the moment the poem was reprinted in traditional print form. An echo of Paz's awareness of (and, I dare say, anxiety about) this loss can be heard in the letter he wrote to Emir Rodríguez Monegal (April 19, 1967), editor of the journal *Mundo Nuevo*, as the poem was also being printed in Mexico. He pointed out, as instructions to print the poem, the need for several-sized fonts and more page centering than was normally done for poems published by the journal. "Si Ud. lee el poema," he warned, "verá que no se trata de caprichos tipográficos" (If you read the poem you'll see these are no typographical whims).[7] Of course, traditional print happens to be the way most readers today know "Blanco." And yet, Paz's concern for its material production was evident at least one year before publication of *Eastern Slope*.

The same concern surfaces in yet another letter of his (January 25, 1968) that topped fifteen months of correspondence with Joaquín Diez Canedo, the Mexican (and first) publisher of "Blanco." Reacting to what appears to be Diez Canedo's misgivings about the finished product—which to a stodgy Spaniard must have seemed weird, to say the least—he wrote: "It's not exactly a *luxury* edition: it's a *functional* edition, aimed at incorporating into the text the material part of the book. I dare say that its typography [*la disposición tipográfica*] constitutes a first reading of the text. The material difficulties of handling it are the equivalent of the language difficulties that every poetic text places before readers."[8]

Yet a second level of material experience appears in the poem's indeterminacy: the reader's choice of various readings as shown in, though not exhaustively contained by, the directions that appear at the end. In the later *Eastern Slope* version of "Blanco," the directions appear at the head of the poem, and for good reason. According to that note—which proves, among other things, that Paz had in mind an open work—there are at least six ways of reading "Blanco": (1) as a single text, (2) reading the center, (3) left column by itself, (4) right column by itself, (5) reading the left and right columns together, and (6) reading the six center sections together with the left and right columns. Nine years later, in a lecture at El Colegio Nacional, Paz himself increased the number of possible readings to fourteen, or rather six sections and fourteen poems, and also proposed the structure of a mandala. Mandalas, as we know, are visual symbolic representations of the universe that are common in Asian cultures. Paz's own mandala had one entrance and one exit—ruled over, respectively, by silence and the color white—plus four intermediate sections with corresponding colors, elements, cardinal points, and faculties. In my essay, however, I disagreed with this count and identified up to twenty-two possible readings, a figure that can actually be increased if we consider the poem's "modular form," to use John M. Fein's useful term. A modular reading allows us to vary the design by manipulating the poem's interchangeable parts. That is, in reading "Blanco" we can opt not to follow the reader directions and simply fold the strip, build our Lego so to speak, whichever way we wish in order to generate our own text.

In the same note attached to *Eastern Slope*, Paz draws the difference between what he calls "temporal order, the form that the poem's course adopts: its discourse," and "spatial order: different parts spread out like mandala regions, colors, symbols and figures."[9] Thus, we certainly can, on this basis, make up our own text. And, there is yet another compelling reason for having the poem proceed as it does: the poem has an order, a logic, an argument, and, of course, a goal or target: *blanco*. Elsewhere, Paz called this "head to toe" composition "fundamental"; it was, in fact, the same order he would follow whenever he gave public readings of the poem, including on the 1995 DVD on "Blanco" that he and Marie José Paz produced.[10] What this meant, ultimately, was that, beyond whatever permutations the poem's spatial order or modular form could generate, the reader appears to have two broad sets of options: either pursue a Western, ironic reading, where we follow directions, or follow an Eastern, analogical reading, where we simply flow with the text.

I mentioned earlier that in 1969, with the inclusion of "Blanco" in *Eastern Slope*, the reader directions shifted from the tail end of the poem to its head. The shift thereby eliminated the physical unfolding of the continuous strip; it also restricted, though not lost totally, the text's modular potential: no longer could the reader perform permutations through modular shifts. On the other hand, the reader could still go through the six alternate readings, which, according to Paz, could amount to as many as fourteen (and, according to Santí, twenty-two). Temporal order, then, won over spatial order, though not completely: the "head to toe," or "fundamental and basic" reading, won out, a reading that the 1969 note, attempting perhaps to make up for the loss of the long-strip format, described further as a ritual, procession, or pilgrimage. Changing the location of the reader directions from the tail end to the head also revealed something else, albeit indirectly. If the reader directions were in fact a guide to reading—as happens, for example, in Julio Cortázar's *Rayuela*—why, then, in the first edition were those directions placed at the tail end rather than at the head?

The obvious answer is that this was the whole point of an Eastern reading: as readers we are supposed to go with the flow, unaided by (Western) instructions. A less obvious answer, however, is the one that the poem's best readers, notably Eliot Weinberger, the translator of "Blanco" into English, and the late Mexican poet Manuel Ulacia have proposed: "Blanco" is actually a reversible text. We can read it in either of two ways. In the first, we start at the end and read toward the top; the first lines would be "La irrealidad de lo mirado / da realidad a la Mirada" (The unreality of the seen / give reality to the seeing); the last word would be "Blanco," the title. In this reverse (actually upward) reading, a different ritual takes place: the gradual ascent of the *kundalini*, instinctual or libidinal energy, through the seven *chakras* of the yogic or Tantric body, which the textual body of "Blanco" is meant to represent. Weinberger explains this as a paradoxical movement: "'Blanco,' which necessarily must be read downwards can be viewed, waxing bold, like a diagram of the chakras in reverse. . . . Thus the kundalini ascends at the same time that the poem descends through the [other] chakras." Ulacia, in turn, went even further by identifying two additional aspects of this reading: first, the six sections of the center column of

"Blanco" represent those six *chakras* (the seventh, which signifies the illumination of emptiness, lies of course outside language); second, the double stanzas of the center column represent the two *kundalini* channels, *rasana* and *lalana*, which correspond to the masculine and feminine principles. They symbolically run up and down, left and right, of the Tantric body, and they channel libidinal energy. Thus, as we read upward, the last word is "*Blanco*"; but as we read downward, the last word is "*Mirada*": "*the seeing*." But be it up or down, we end up in the same place: the *sixth* chakra at the forehead, "the color of which," according to Weinberger, alluding to Buddhist doctrine, "is transparency": "Transparency is all that remains," goes one of the more prominent mantras of "Blanco."[11]

No doubt you have noted that while describing the second level of material experience, the poem's indeterminacy, I have also been hinting at the third: the Tantric ritual that makes up the poem's narrative and that we could otherwise call its diegesis. To delve further into the particulars of Tantric doctrine would take us far afield. More pertinent for our immediate purposes would be simply to limit ourselves to the paradox that sustains it and that I have otherwise described as radical absence by means of radical presence.

Paz himself, in a number of writings, referred to the paradox of how Tantra, being an extension of Buddhism, is itself a new and exaggerated attempt to reabsorb, within the great critical and metaphysical negation of Mahayana, yogic, bodily, and primal elements. Thus, in ritual copulation the yogi must avoid ejaculation, a practice that has two goals: (1) to deny the reproductive function of sexuality and (2) to transform semen into the thought of enlightenment. Thus Tantrism employs ritual sexual intercourse, among other physical transgressions (which can include bingeing, intoxication, defecation, and vomiting). It does so as "immersion into chaos, into the original source of life," on the one hand, and ascetic practice, a purification of the senses and of the mind, on the other. The procedure is meant to reach into the annulment of world and self. In "Blanco," the erotic ritual appears in its central column, each of whose sections is divided in turn into two stanzas in what constitutes a counterpoint between erotic ritual (on the left) and modes of knowledge (on the right). In the poem's sixth section, the literal climax, the two stanzas colored in red and black join together typographically in an ideogrammic representation of the couple's orgasmic union. The climax also coincides thematically, diegetically, with the speaker's attainment of language. That is, linguistic germination (poetic achievement, lifting of the writer's block) occurs simultaneously with the couple's orgasmic climax.

The above description of the three levels of material experience—what I should like to call the levels of physical reading, interpretation, and diegesis—is actually meant as a preface to my main point. It is also a preface to a new modest proposal regarding "Blanco," to which I shall now devote the last brief section of this chapter. Although I have already stated my main point, I shall clarify it further. By the time the reader reaches the concluding, ninth section of "Blanco," beginning with the key lines

In the center
Of the world of the body of the spirit
The crevice The splendor

two contradictory issues have taken place. The first is that we (speaker and reader) have arrived at the verge of illumination through emptiness; "the crevice" is the poem's metaphor for this experience. The second issue is that we have become aware of emptiness by virtue of an earlier, more radical, and opposite experience: the complex materiality we have gone through by virtue of reading, interpretation, and diegesis. Indeed, the "crevice," this crack or slit through which both speaker and reader now perceive "splendor" (where world, body, and spirit become one and the same), also constitutes the metaphor for both the woman's vulva (worshipped in Tantric ritual, experienced in the poem) and the fissure through which we transcend relativism. That is, the "crevice" is both physical object and metaphysical concept. According to Paz, the "crevice" is the tear that allows us to experience poetry, "the other shore." That we are at a higher stage of consciousness is signaled further by the poem's line "in the center," where "center" refers not only to the reader's return to the poem's center column. It also alludes to "the Way of the Center," the name given historically to *Madhyamika*, the middle road of Buddhist relativity that was reconceptualized and refined by Nagarjuna, the master of this "central" tendency that proclaims an emptiness that neither affirms nor denies the world.[12]

What I here call a higher stage of consciousness represents merely an inadequate conceptual shortcut for understanding what that "central" or middle way entails. For once we become aware of such relativity and our language names emptiness, if indeed everything is emptiness, then the proposition "everything is emptiness" is itself empty. The world tears open and "splendor" appears through the "crevice." The end of "Blanco" thus describes metaphorically a logical operation: the world becomes meaningful by means of acknowledging its emptiness, an acknowledgment that turns against itself and therefore dissolves the assertion. Far from fleeing the world, then, as some Western readings of the poem wish to do, "Blanco" returns to the world and plunges into all its relative relations. The first of these is the link between "world" and "word," thus the cryptic lines "if the world is real, the word is unreal," "yes and no, two syllables in love," etc. By this point, we have reached the stage of silence after the word. But because by now we have also learned that the only thing worth saying cannot be said, the poem resorts to acknowledging and celebrating the world.

Pere Gimferrer, whose early, sensitive reading of "Blanco" has been the basis of many interpretations, was wrong, I think, when he limited the poem's anecdotal content (what I call the celebration of the world) to the "steps heard in the other room," to which the speaker refers in this last section. While Gimferrer does attribute this anecdote correctly to the speaker's woman companion, I would argue that this is hardly the only other anecdote to which the poem refers.[13] In fact, the poem makes constant, if elliptical, references to many other objects, events, and experiences to which the speaker responds as he attempts to write the poem—for example, the "sunflower" and "lamp" of the first section, the "insect" that flops through the manuscript pages; the Livingstone diary that happens to be on his desk and from which he quotes, the thunder and lightning heard in a looming storm; the "amethyst ring" he turns on his finger; the music heard in the next room along with the woman's steps. All of these everyday material events, objects, and circumstances are, in fact, anecdotal and constitute what Paz elsewhere calls the experience of otherness. As we know, Paz first described otherness in a long, lyrical reflection in the essay "Signs in Rotation" (1965); but in his written reaction to drafts of my old essay, never before made public, he drove the point further. Otherness was the stuff "Blanco" was made of:

> *Otherness* designates everyday life . . . in its radical strangeness. . . . It is the stuff of poetry, from its origins until today. . . . It is the experience of being in the world, being here and now. On one extreme, Otherness borders with religion and philosophy; on the other, with everyday life. Otherness is . . . the central source for Blanco, which is a carnal poem, a love poem. . . . Yet, the experience of Otherness is unsayable; it alludes to a reality beyond words and that only silence can name. (Poetry can name it, too, but only by alluding to it.) Each true poem, be it a haiku or a long poem, is a window open onto infinity, onto the Otherness that makes us up.[14]

We would not be wrong in viewing Paz's attempt in "Blanco" to find equivalents in Western poetic language to the experience of empty illumination that he found in Tantric Buddhism. Indeed, this is the central goal of Paz's mature thought on poetry and poetics during the late 1960s and 1970s. The problem, of course, is that no such actual equivalent exists in Western experience, which makes the experience of "Blanco" hypothetical at best. How can we represent emptiness, precisely that which excludes expression and representation? Paz's technical compromise, so to speak, was therefore to attempt a material equivalent by making paper the literal ground of absence, or as he once noted about the 1969 reprint version: "*Blanco*'s typography and binding wanted to underscore not so much the presence of the text as the space that sustains it: that which makes writing and reading possible, and where all writing and reading end."[15] Yet despite such monumentally daring experimentation, it is also evident that from the outset Paz became aware of the inadequacy of that compromise. For years he sought ways to resolve that inadequacy, or at least improve on it. He sought it, first, through public readings of the poem. As early as May 2, 1967, he told editor Diez Canedo that the reading he was planning in Mexico City would be "special": "partly recorded, either with my voice or with two actors, plus a very brief audition of modern music in which language would appear more for its sounds than for its meaning."[16] Years later in those pre-digital days, he wanted to work with the artist Vicente Rojo and produce a film based on "Blanco." In a March 6, 1968, letter he described that project as "a screening of the book (and of the act of reading it) . . . that would combine dynamically letters, spoken words, visual and hearing sensations and the different senses. In other words: the transfer of an interior subjective movement (reading) onto an exterior objective movement (film screening)." He added, and reiterated barely eight months later in another letter to Rojo, that "letters would appear on the screen, either moving or upon a moving background with changing colors; other times, upon the empty screen there would appear only colors and abstract forms and the audience would hear the words without reading the text."[17] The film with Vicente Rojo was never made. Paz himself made it in 1995. Finally, in this long list there was a stage version of "Blanco," whose idea also dates from 1968, when Paz first proposed it to the Mexican director José Luis Ibáñez and even sent him a script.[18] Twenty-three years later Paz would even give a slightly different version of that script to Vicente Molina Foix, the distinguished Spanish writer who at the time was director of Madrid's National Theatre, for a staging that unfortunately never took place. Today we have the good fortune to have both the 1995 DVD version plus a third staging and DVD, both made recently by the Catalan artist Fredric Amat.[19]

All of the avatars of this complex poem demonstrate, I think, that, in addition to its supple materiality, there remained another element, the strange matter of its performativity. It was as if Paz had been the first to become aware that it was only through its fleeting performance that one could capture the central, paradoxical core of "Blanco": the presence of absence.

2

"Blanco" and *Transblanco*

Modern and Post-Utopian

JOÃO ADOLFO HANSEN

Paz composed "Blanco" in New Delhi in 1966; Haroldo de Campos translated it in Austin, Texas, in 1981; and, we continue to discuss and engage with these texts today. Something decisive took place in these intervals of time: if the literal meaning of the poem and its translation have remained practically the same, their aesthetic and political meaning have not. With this in mind, I wish to explore some articulations of "Blanco" and perform a small exercise of memory, recalling some useful elements of Brazilian concretism to think of how Campos proposes his translation as a post-utopian practice and how we might deal with the poem today.

In "Blanco," the image of the body as a peregrination gives us back the image of the body as writing. Speaking at the University of São Paulo, Paz claimed that he had transformed time into space. To reach this target (*blanco*) and this space (*blanco*), he condenses historical references of different periods. There are, for example, the Aztecs of Mexico-Tenochtitlán-Texcoco (e.g., the utterance "I am the dust of this mud"), the Aztec flower war, the hieroglyphics of blood of human sacrifice, Mexico under Spanish colonial rule, and modern Mexico. The poem integrates them into metaphors of Tibetan Buddhism, which Paz employs as a matrix for topics he arranges in the form of a mandala. Within this mandala, the four paths of the enunciation find expression through four colors (yellow, red, green, and blue) that converge with the four elements (fire, water, earth, and air) and the four faculties (sense, perception, imagination, and understanding). The "self" passes through the continuum of various illusory states of existence and reaches enlightenment through the sexual conjunction of the *muchacha* (girl) and the man, corresponding to Nairatmya, woman-wisdom, *prajna* or not-self, and the Buddha Hevajra, the enlightened man-instrument, articulated through an epigraph taken from the Hevajra Tantra, an eighth- to ninth-century Buddhist text.

As we know, the medium of the Buddhist Tantra is the vision of the continuity of illumination in every human state and condition, and also its discontinuity. In Tantra, the medium of the vision of this continuity presupposes the four basic statements of Buddhism: (1) everything is without essence, (2) everything is transitory, (3) everything is illusory, and (4) nirvana is a blessing. In the text of the Hevajra Tantra, the mandala imitated by Paz has a white center as the base of the throne where Hevajra and Nairatmya are unified through sex, symbolizing the final elimination of oppositions. With the lateral expansions of left and right in the central discourse of the poem, the expansions that refer to the four colors (yellow, red, green, blue) corresponding to the four faculties of the soul simultaneously enlightened (sense, perception, imagination, understanding), Paz emulates the Hevajra Tantra, making the mandala also complete itself in the sexual act seen as a vision emptied of visibility, which gives reality to the vision of the poem by the reader.

In his book *Dzogchen: The Self-Perfected State*, the Tibetan monk Namkhai Norbu writes on the medium of the Tantra practice in a way that helps one understand the movements of "Blanco":

> The practice of the Tantra has two phases: the development stage and the "perfectioning" stage. The first phase consists of the stage of gradual visualization of the mandala, beginning with the seed syllable of the principal divinity and the syllables of the four elements. When the imaginary creation of the mandala is complete, whilst maintaining the visualization of oneself transformed into the form of the central divinity, one recites the mantra. In this phase, one works a great deal with the imaginative faculty of the mind, trying to develop to the maximum one's capacity to visualize. The second phase, the "perfectioning" stage, focuses on the visualization of the internal mandala of the centers (*chakra*) and channels (*nadi*) and on concentration on the syllables of the mantra, which turns without interruption around the central seed syllable. At the end of the practice session, both the external and internal mandalas are integrated in the dimension of the body, in the enlightened speech and mind of the practitioner. The final result of the practice is that pure vision manifests itself without depending any longer on visualization, becoming part of one's natural clarity. Thus, one realizes the total state of reintegration of pure vision with impure vision, the *Mahamudra*, the "great symbol" in which samsara and nirvana are indissolubly united.[1]

Paz composes "Blanco" as a metaphor of the Mahamudra, the reintegration of the pure with the impure vision, extracting from the Hevajra Tantra the third and fourth initial words, "seed" and "latent." In the Hevajra Tantra, they signify the nucleus of the energy sleeping in the chest of every human being. The latent seed emerges out of the passions of the soul that the practitioner takes as means for exercises that dissolve *samsara* (appearance) into the nothingness of nirvana, made immanent as a dissolution of the self and of all the sensitive and intelligible oppositions. In the poem, the word "seed" is a metaphor for the word that forms the sensation, the perception, the imagination, and the thought. The poem presents the thought sexually, as the phallus that penetrates the organ of the word, eliminating from it subjective expression, reference, and signification. In this way, it achieves purification without speech, without an object, and without signification. As the Hevajra Tantra puts it: "The transparency is what is left," retaken in the final segment, in which statements and their negations unite, achieving space as a vacuity—one in which body, thought, and word are undone.

The poetic word of Paz has its origin in Mexico, and he suggests that the river of its discourse is *rojo*, a hieroglyph of the blood carved onto the chest of a fallen Mexico. It shows the political, critical, and modern function of Paz's poetry: to polish the bones of historical experience as an expiation of the violence that triggers the elimination of contradictions, rousing the silences in the final transparency, in which the subject of the enunciation and its historical determinations are annulled. The same thought presents the reader as a reciprocity of seeing and being seen: it is my creation that which I see / I am the creation of what I see. And, just as in Tantra, Paz conceives of the imagination as a means of visualizing the end envisioned by the word: the imagination is the unreality of what is seen, which gives reality to the vision of the emptiness of the representations of the reader in the leftovers of the poem written in the language of the exterior.

A metaphor for Buddhism, the emptiness of "Blanco" is homologous to the effects of emptiness in modern symbolical practices such as the poetic experience of Stéphane Mallarmé in the "Crise de vers," "Un coup de dés," and *Igitur*, and of the emptiness of plastic constructivisms such as the concrete art of Doesburg, the suprematism of Malevitch, and the Brazilian concretism of the 1950s and 1960s. The two epigraphs taken from the Hevajra Tantra and the *Sonnet en yx* of Mallarmé thus condense and guide the legibility of "Blanco" as a modern and internationalist discourse that transforms diverse layers of history, tending to outdo in the form the expression of the subject, the designation of the reference, and the mimetic signification of the concept. The emptiness of nirvana accomplished by the metaphorization of Tantric enlightenment is analogous to the atopic place of language given over by the epigraph of Mallarmé. As a modern fiction, the poem dissolves the imaginary of representation, for it stages the imaginary of the symbolic as the transposition and the structure that form the *blanco*, the whiteness of the topological space of signs. When Paz associates Tantra with Mallarmé, he arranges the time sequence of these enunciations as a discontinuous parataxis of historically diverse discourses that converge. The effect of this convergence is that one sees the whiteness of the paper not just as a simple support for words but also as the emptiness of the achieved goal and the emergence of the great Other. The poetic effect of emptiness in the presence of whiteness as enlightenment also makes present the phantasmal body of language. In this sense, there is nothing to interpret, since there is no Other of the Other and the interpretation would replace what the poem is dissolving. But the reading may be seen as a poetic redoing of the complication of the syntactical intersections in which the word associates with what comes before and after and is simultaneously displaced from its position, alluding—in the event of its apparition—to the silence of the structure that it insists upon as other.

We know from Saussure that a distinctive feature of the phonological is that it marks the signifier as the presence of the absence in all systems of language: "a" is "a" because it is not "b," and so on. We know that the nonsense of metaphor derives from the simultaneous superposition of features that apparently could not be there; we know that, in metonymy, it is the feature that appears, pointing to the connection of the chain. Therefore, when I speak, the subject pronoun "I" also speaks itself in the third person, since the language is thought through the difference of pronouns independently of the tiny substantialist imaginary of the "self" accomplished as an effect of it. I think I am thinking, and something thinks of itself inside my body thinking of me as the energy of the seed of the Hevajra Tantra. Here, recalling Mallarmé, "Ma pensée s'est pensée" (My thinking is thinking) is a poetic program that can be related metaphorically to the latent seed of Tantra in order to make the reader see the phonological differential in the whitenesses of the spaces.

To avoid the randomness of free associations of the differences in metaphors and the randomness of the mad flow triggered by metonymy, Mallarmé calculates the negativity of the linguistic difference as a syntactic deviation that figures its atopic interval as the space of a theater impossible of any theater, since it does not figure forth things in movement but the movement itself of difference from sign to sign. Metaphorically, whiteness in Mallarmé's poetry and in art since Cézanne can be called an Other, a black hole, quantum physics, *Rien*, *Néant*, Nothing, God, One, Enlightenment, *satori*, nirvana, zen, Zohar, *maná*, negative mystics, and other metaphors. In the beginning of Christianity, Pseudo-Dionysius spoke of apophasis, the technique of negative figuring forth the impossibility of figuring the absoluteness of God and of the angelical hierarchy that we find in the metaphysics of light in Dante's *Paradiso*. In the twentieth century, Ludwig Wittgenstein spoke of a God whose existence is only relational, functionally accomplished as an exterior signification of a contingent act of speech. Michel Foucault spoke of the language of the exterior; Michel de Certeau spoke of mystics as the language of the Other, incorporating Jacques Lacan. And Jean-François Lyotard resumed the sublime of Immanuel Kant's conceptualization, which had in turn resumed the *Perì hypsous* of Longinus, and spoke of the insignificant *bêtise* of postmodern art as a negative representation of the impossibility of figuring forth reality in postindustrial societies. But in "Crise de vers," Mallarmé had already spoken of the elocutionary disappearance of the subject and the hole of language, star/disaster, whose emptied form he also looked for in the Parnassian poets—Gautier, Banville—as the exactness of the arabesque drawing of the prismatic divisions of the Idea that announce the neutral exterior of language without self, without thing, without final signification, the lace of Hamlet's collar, *rien au delà*, the pierced body of language as difference, at last as space and the elocutionary disappearance of the full self in the false appearance of the present of the broken crystals in Hugo's china cabinet, such as in the book of the dead *Elbhenon*: Mallarmé, *le mâle armé* of the cogito.

Mallarmé's experiences of the concretism of Doesburg, Albers, and Max Bill and of Malevitch's suprematism (present in Paz) are also central components of Brazilian concrete poetry. The fundamental difference is that Paz's poem does not abolish the discourse of history, unlike concrete poetry, for which historical reference is above all formal, assumed in the reduction of the poetic to the word "verbivocovisually," defined as an object on its own as a synthesis resultant from a supposed historical evolution of artistic forms. Because it sees the consideration of the word as a matrix form of invention, "Blanco" co-naturally opens itself to the procedures of Haroldo de Campos's translation, which, in the 1980s, resumed the concretist procedures with a new aesthetic and political meaning, which he called "post-utopic."

Evidently enough, what is said in "Blanco" is not the discourse of Buddhism or of philosophy, linguistics, or history, since it is singular: a modern fiction calculatedly designed as an act of dissolution of the imaginary of the representation, the imaginary that produces the reader as a necessity for producing interpretations. Mallarmé insistently speaks in his letters of this act that dissolves the imaginary of representation: it is above all a critical act, and Sollers spoke of the *mâle armé*'s political economy of the sign, the Master who descends to the river of death because he sees the arbitrary of the symbolic and disappears, looking at himself in the mirror to guarantee the body, Mallarmé *septuor*, the Ursa minor. The lineage of "Blanco" is Mallarmean, modern, critical of representation. The speech that interprets the poem's empty space easily transforms itself into animated discourse through the mystics of the negative presence, as also happens with Heideggerian uses of Saussure and Jakobson, pointing to the unveiling of Being and other such paths leading nowhere. It is possible to make metaphorical associations that extend the signification of the poem into the immanent lateral space of its structure; but such associations are disputable when the metaphor overlaps with the metaphysical imaginary of the reader and bleeds into the material codification of the text, assuming a first stance, profound and high, that understands the poem to be the experience of a certain transcendence.

The figuring forth of difference can be materially thought of as a poetic procedure that waves to the infinitude of combinations as the fiction of an autonomized language of any *parole*, the language of the exterior of which Foucault speaks. Representation presupposes the motivation or the substantial correspondence among subject, sign, and thing. Poetic representation before Mallarmé—perhaps before Baudelaire—is characterized by the unity of the cogito, by the motivated adequacy of the sign to the concept, by the natural relation of the concept and the sign with a reason presumed as a given in the things themselves. Presuming this equivalence, the discourse of representation is the expression of interiority, the designation of exteriority, and the signification of ideality. As expression, designation, and signification, discourse is founded on transcendental meanings or on one transcendental meaning risen above all as a first and final meaning—such as God or Being—which grounds the unity of the self, of objective reality, and of the sign.

Representation is smooth and without fractures; when there is crisis, it does not lie with representation but with the things and to the self. For this reason, in the poetry of representation there is a mimetic proportion between the distances, greater or smaller, more or less adequate, of similitude, which define discourse, and the mimetic unities presumed, which are revealed, represented, or in the process of being represented by discourse. To speak of emptiness in "Blanco," we presume the exterior of all this, the negativity of the differential of the sign as its assumption and horizon. The poem's title indicates the modern myth of the topological space of signs, which the enunciation makes effective by cutting the white space of the page while it eliminates itself, becoming the presence itself of the absence of white in the space of the page. In the prismatic divisions of eroticism, of the four colors corresponding to the four elements and to sensation, perception, imagination, and thought, the mandala of Paz spins around an absent center, being generated by the seed-word of the initial speech act, always as something existing because it insists on logorrhoea. Paz knows that, since Hugo's crystals have been broken in the poetical china cabinet of "Crise de vers," the fracturing of the subject is exposed as an inhabited language that carves its hieroglyphs in space. Poetry is no more the expression of the "I," which dissolves itself with the Romanticism that became impossible just like the dust of the mud in Tenochtitlán. "Pas sentiment ni esprit: neutralité" (Not sentiment nor spirit: neutrality), says Mallarmé. And since he does not presume any rationality of the real, no order pre-inscribed in things, poetry is not the smooth designation of the exterior, and realism is impossible: "désolé de l'humanité," which dissolves itself in the pieces of speech dripping in the noiseless river of bloody histories. And the inequality of signifier and signified, the unmotivation and the arbitrariness of the sign *denué de toute signification que de présence*, demonstrates that God or Being is just a meaning among others, and that it was merely transformed into the foremost meaning.

Poetically, using once more the metaphor of broken crystals, the metaphors of Buddhism and of Mallarmé used by Paz place into relief the impossibility of thinking of a continent, of a cup, Mallarmé's *fiole*, form, as a mimetic, reflexive, analogous or verisimilar adequacy of the truth of any substantial content: wine, I, real, God. It is marvelous that Mallarmé does in fact see the material invisibility of language in a metaphysical formula, *néant*—"void." Paz sharpens the silence of this invisibility, and, as we read in "Blanco," transparency is everything and all that is left. Such transparency is obscure to those who read "Blanco" by the light of representation and presuming the unities of representation; but it is clear by the light of the poem's own assumptions, without a first, without height, without profundity, without interiority, as poetry strongly marked by the events of history and by the history of Western poetical forms.

It is superficial poetry, if the term "superficial" were not yet so compromised with representation. Just as in Carlos Drummond de Andrade's *Claro enigma*, which quotes Mallarmé directly in the poems and indirectly in the epigraph (which cites Valéry), in "Blanco" the traditional semantic verisimilitude grounded in truth has vanished. What is left is the syntactic verisimilitude of the effect of his throw of the dice, as the fiction of the Tantric continuum. In the world of representation, poetry is the invention of discourses like the presumed unities of self, reality, and meaning. When these unities are dissolved, differences emerge. In "Blanco," as Deleuze has said, it is the differences that become similar, not the similarities that differ: the Hevajra Tantra, the Nahuatl speech of Nezahualcoyotl (a fifteenth-century king of Texcoco), Mallarmé, concretism, suprematism. In the modern poetry of Mallarmé and Paz—and it is necessary to include here the painting of Cézanne—it is this *folie utile / folie nécessaire* of a Beatrice/Nairatmya of the structure that systematically eliminates the expression, designation, and signification of mimesis grounded on the games of similitude. As Mallarmé says, to enunciate is to produce, and "Blanco" is poetry produced as the "abolit bibelot d'inanité sonore," where the absent flower of every white bouquet alludes to the pressure of the signifier.[2] Pressure, yes, since language is an inhuman body, maybe a constellation, shiny spots of contingent sense in the black hole of death, occupying every scene of the poem as a theater impossible of a theater in which nothing is being acted, except the movement of the differential of the signifier spatialized in whiteness as the movement of movement, mimesis of mimesis.

Haroldo de Campos's translation is given as a poetical happening, freezing the temporality of enunciation as a pictorial space, enabling us to see the fantastic body of language. "Blanco" is not a concretist poem, as I have said, but its postulate that word and language are poetic topics, its syntactic discontinuity, the quotation and condensation of multicultural references united by the interpretive "emptiness" and "nothing" as a metaphor of the topic of the topological space of language, makes the poem co-natural with the Brazilian concretism of the 1960s and also with the post-utopian project of Haroldo de Campos's poetic invention and translation in the 1980s.

In 1958, Augusto de Campos, Haroldo de Campos, and Décio Pignatari intended to update the Brazilian intellect through the invention of concretist poetry, which they defined in constructivist terms in the first version of the *Plano piloto da poesia concreta*, published in the magazine *Noigandres*. An avant-garde intervention, concretist poetry was destructive and opposed above all else the "choir of the contented," a formula invented by the modernist Oswald de Andrade to classify those associated with traditional art forms. To conquer the space opened up by his intervention, the concretist neo-avant-garde began to dispute the aesthetic and political hegemony of Brazilian literary terrain, disqualifying the neo-Parnassian poetry of the so-called Generation of 1945 and competing mainly with the University of São Paulo (USP) group, which was then extracting, as it does even now, the dividends of the symbolic capital accumulated by the critic Antonio Candido. The poetic objects of the neo-avant-garde were ferociously self-referential; at the same time, they reached for the universality of the literary field, proclaiming themselves the *ultra non plus* of aesthetic value. The neo-avant-garde eliminated the particularity of its negative moment, claiming itself to be the utmost norm and horizon of aesthetic value. Different from the group at USP, which was teleologically organized around the idealist notion of *Bildung*, the concretist group was anti-romantic and anti-expressionist in defining theoretical assumptions, technical procedures, and the aesthetic value of its objects, though many of the formulas incessantly repeated by the group—such as "historical evolution of the forms" and "critical nationalism open to the universal"—were also committed to the teleology of the national and the progress of the arts. Its anti-romanticism was not immediately political, as was the romanticism or the modernism of the sociological *Bildung* group. It was above all an aesthetic anti-romanticism, critical of the dominant expressive realism of the canon. The members of the group called themselves concretists, since the "-ism" of concretism was an obvious sign of academicism. When the moment of intervention had passed, and the group claimed to be the moral portent of the new and put forward diverse "neos," it became objectively concretist, like a self-contradictory and academic avant-garde that lasted for more than thirty years.

We know that Doesburg used the term "concretism" to oppose concrete and abstract. Max Bense recalled with Hegel that abstract is always something that presumes something else by which it is abstracted; concrete means something on its own. Doesburg used the term in this sense, to give meaning to the materiality of the line, of the geometrical surface and the rhythmical relation between the colors, in opposition to the illusionism of mimetic art. For the concrete plastic artists of São Paulo in the 1950s, the opposition concrete/abstract or concrete/representative was the main one. They defined concretism as a constructivist rationality that presumed the progress of what they called the historical evolution of forms since Cézanne, since the cubism of Braque and Picasso and the intellectual reduction of the plastic materials accomplished by Mondrian and Malevitch. They opposed themselves to the strong expressionist matrix that then characterized Brazilian plastic arts and were then the enemies of abstract painting. Concretist painting eliminated representation as a mediation interposed in the plastic form; in a homologous way, concretist poetry claimed that it was surpassing what it called the "old formal syllogistic and discursive foundation of the verse," replacing it with what Augusto de Campos called the syntactic and perspectivistic arrangement of the word on the blank page made according to the opposing form or depth of the Gestalt.

In a book on neo-concretism in Rio de Janeiro, Ronaldo Brito recalls that plastic concretism had proposed the systematic exploration of the serial form and the mechanical movement of time, defining itself as a nonpsychological intentionality, strictly optical and sensorial, opposed to the representation and to the informal abstractionism.[3] As a work that placed emphasis on its own formal principles, concretist art was an aesthetic mediation of the optical and sensorial possibilities defined by Gestalt theory. The concrete painters of São Paulo were an orthodox group, and they uniformly opposed the heterodoxy of the neo-concrete group of Rio, mainly regarding the function of color. The concrete artists of São Paulo, such as Waldemar Cordeiro, suggested that painting should be a pure serial and rhythmic opposition of white/black, claiming that color was a subjectivist residue that induced psychologism. In both groups—the concretists of São Paulo and the neo-concretists of Rio—the political in art emerged by presenting the painter, the sculptor, and the poet as industrial designers whose horizon was the modern rationalization of the Brazilian social milieu. Perhaps they knew that Brazil was a class-based society in which the bourgeoisie was preparing the dictatorship of 1964 in order to radicalize the process of a conservative modernization, a process that dominates the country even now. They believed, with a certain Enlightenment naïveté, that the alteration of the perceptive habits of the artistic form would fatally trigger a change in the spectator's political habits. They passed over the realist Lukács. From Adorno, they perhaps kept the idea of a negative rationalization of form that, refusing representation, should be sufficient to change the way spectators saw their surroundings: "Without revolutionary form, there is no revolutionary art." The concretist poets added Maiakovski to the *Plano piloto da poesia concreta* in 1961; however, the term "revolutionary" had nothing to do with Marxist dialectics and class struggle. It simply meant formal innovation in a society where right-wing oligarchs, assisted by the Roman Catholic Church and the United States, steered every other social institution toward conservative modernization.

The concrete neo-avant-garde selected its own Brazilian predecessors, suggesting an alternative canon. Very schematically, the first Romantic Brazilian authors of Gonçalves de Magalhães's group (1836), and of the Brazilian Historical and Geographical Institute (1838), suggested that Brazilian literature should be a "civilized indigene," adapting European forms to local material to represent the unified physical and social reality of a country recently independent from Portugal. Ever since the Romantics, the greater part of Brazilian fiction has been characterized by a realist concern with documenting the national. It was applied between 1836 and 1870 as local color in the poetry of Magalhães and Gonçalves Dias and in the novels of Alencar; it was translated by the end of the nineteenth century as the representation of races, climate, and environment by the positivist science of realist and naturalist authors such as Aluísio Azevedo and Euclides da Cunha; it was resumed in the artistic and political movements committed to discovering the country in the Week of Modern Art of 1922 and in the critical realism of the Northeastern novels in 1930. The documented representation of what is national tended to relegate the imagination and experimentalism to a secondary position, and that is when it did not openly seek to eliminate or suppress them.

The claim made by Mario de Andrade, head of the modernist movement of 1922, is paradigmatic: it is indispensable to avoid Góngora, it is indispensable to avoid Mallarmé. In his *Formação da literatura brasileira* (1959), Antonio Candido gives continuity to the Romantic-modernist project through his Enlightenment-inspired and openly sociological interpretation of literature, based on the German idealist notion of *Bildung*. Candido excludes the so-called baroque from the literary canon, dating the supposed origin of the organic body of Brazilian literature back to the poetry of the Arcadian poets of Minas Gerais and Rio de Janeiro, from the end of the eighteenth century. His view still dominates the majority of language and literature courses at Brazilian universities, and it has been naturalized as evident, not read as a specific interpretative model but as the truth of reality represented in interpreted texts.

But the best of Brazilian fiction is that which shows imagination and experimentalism. For instance, after 1881, Machado de Assis wrote such novels and short stories, bringing back procedures of Menippean satire that Ludovico Ariosto, Miguel de Cervantes, and Lawrence Sterne had taken from Lucian of

Samosata. In 1928, Mario de Andrade published a rhapsodic novel, *Macunaíma*. Oswald de Andrade produced the cubic-futurist experiment of the *Memórias sentimentais de João Miramar* (1922) and poems in the style of Apollinaire in *Pau-Brasil* (1924); he launched the anthropophagic manifesto in 1928 and published the anti-novel *Serafim Ponte Grande* in 1933, besides writing plays that would be essential to the *tropicalista* movement of the 1960s. Between 1940 and 1970, João Guimarães Rosa and Clarice Lispector invented new languages, and Brazil's three greatest modern poets—Drummond, Murilo Mendes, and João Cabral de Melo Neto—strongly criticized representation.

Members of the concretist group dedicated themselves to these authors, choosing them and not others as predecessors. For example, Haroldo de Campos wrote his PhD applying Propp's morphology to *Macunaíma*. In several papers and talks, he presented Oswald de Andrade as Brazil's principal modernist author. He talked of Lispector's abstract prose, wrote a key text on Guimarães Rosa's *Meu tio, o Iauaretê*, and wrote many articles on Drummond, Mendes, and Cabral de Melo Neto. He also valued the metalinguistic procedures of Machado de Assis in *Memórias póstumas de Brás Cubas*. Augusto de Campos brought together Guimarães Rosa and Mallarmé. Décio Pignatari analyzed Drummond's poetry in constructivist terms and proposed that the main protagonist of *Dom Casmurro* is the chapter. In 1989, Haroldo de Campos published *O sequestro do barroco: O caso Gregório de Matos*, against what he called, following Derrida and Heidegger, Candido's "metaphysics of subjectivity." At the same time, the concretists were extremely active redefining the canon by republishing forgotten or excluded Brazilian poets such as the Romantics from Maranhão, Sousândrade (*O guesa*) and Odorico Mendes (translator of Homer and Virgil), and the symbolist poet from Bahia, Pedro Kilkerry, suggesting that their inventions were superior to the inventions of the consecrated poets of the canon. References to Peirce's semiotics, to Wiener's theory of information, to Max Bense's aesthetics, to Jakobson's linguistics, to the functionalism of Le Corbusier, to the Bauhaus and the Ulm School, to Brazilian and European concretist poetry, to Malevitch's suprematism, to Arnault Daniel, Marcabru, Guillaume de Poitiers, Dante, John Donne, Hölderlin, Gertrude Stein, Joyce, Pound, Marianne Moore, cummings, Mallarmé, Apollinaire, Ponge, Ungaretti, Ballestrini, Huidobro, Lezama Lima, and so on cross over into the texts produced by the concretist poets, who were always guided by the opposition between formal and informal, nondiscursive and discursive, and so on.

If, as Mondrian used to say, painting is the medium for optically achieving thought, and if every painting is a color thought, the construction of the painting results from the invention of the space rationally controlled by the painter's eye. And when Mondrian is reduced to the obviousness of the materiality of the support, the blank canvas, Malevitch may paint white on white, in a figuration that eliminates the expressive manifestation of the subject, the realist designation of reference, and the signification of the concept. In the heroic time of the end of the 1950s, when concretist artists announced that the verse was dead, the elimination of discursivity also eliminated the "I" of the expressive enunciation. When this moment had passed, they went after Pound's slogan of "make it new" and after notions of translation as transcreation that Walter Benjamin had put forward. Such notions permitted them—now in fact concretists—to continue making great verses through translations of the book of Genesis, Homer, Dante, Provençal poets, John Donne, Mallarmé, Maiakovski, Japanese texts, and so on, transforming them into concrete and concretist texts *avant la lettre*. In a letter to Paz in 1983, Haroldo de Campos remains a concretist when he pejoratively refers to a rhetorical and expressive tradition of Mexican poetry based on metaphor.

In 1984, in "Poesia e modernidade: Da morte da arte à constelação. O poema pós-utópico," Haroldo de Campos proposed that modern poetic projects oriented by the utopia of the future were used up, claiming that the time had come to produce a post-utopian poetry characterized by the plurality of possible poetics as a poetics that would produce temporary syntheses where the only residue of the present would be the critical-dialogical dimension of utopia. The elimination of modern categories and concepts that, at least up to 1980, had guided the reception of Paz's and the concretists' modern poetry could help us think about *Transblanco*. With the notion of "plural history," which, according to Haroldo de Campos, would characterize his present in 1984, he proposed—in a way similar to what Ezra Pound had done in the *Cantos* as a collector of the disarranged broken bits of universal history—poetic practice as an appropriation of a "plurality of pasts" without a previous political or aesthetic determination of the future. In other words, poetry without the utopian dimension of future. Haroldo de Campos stated that concretist poetry was over, but that it had taught him to see transtemporally the concrete of poetry as a global and open process in which the translator would have the function of being the poet of poetry as the poet of the poet or a poet for poets. Defining translation as a critical reading practice—"critical" only in a formal sense, as a reflection on tradition—he stated that it would permit the recombination of the plurality of possible pasts as difference in the post-utopian poem written here and now.

In this sense, Campos's translation of "Blanco" presupposes the radical changes of the concept of historical time determined by capital at the beginning of the 1980s. Such changes make his translation a post-utopian poem, different from Paz's original, which had been a modern poem in 1966. At the same time, the translation maintains theoretical and technical elements in the way that the concretists, in the 1960s, understood the word as the triadic sign of Charles Peirce: a sign of its sonorous-semantic-visual materiality, a sign of the reference, a sign to an addressee as the interpretant of the signification and the poetical function of words. Just like in other translations by Haroldo de Campos, *Transblanco* operates functionally as a Peircian interpretant that explores the sonorous-semantic-spatial materiality of "Blanco," evidencing the virtualities of the configuration of its signification and meaning. His theory of translation is close to what seventeenth-century poets called *emulation*, an imitation that discovers the main predicates of the original text in a witty variation that competes with its symbolic efficacy, partially surpassing it. Haroldo de Campos translates by emulation, according to the meaning given to the term by, for example, Emanuele Tesauro: "I thus call imitation a sagacity with which, when a metaphor or such like flower of the human wit is to you presented, you carefully consider its roots, and, transplanting it in different categories like in a cultivated and fertile ground, you propagate other flowers of the same species, but not the individuals themselves."[4]

Translation as a post-utopian practice is also a polishing of bones, but without giving to the polish the negative trait of a criticism of the present. It is now up to us to discuss what the translation by Haroldo de Campos and the poem by Octavio Paz is and what it means today, when that modern project has been institutionalized as a dead classic in a museum and the emptiness we experience is not the emptiness of Tantra, of Mallarmé, of the plastic arts of the beginning of the twentieth century, of Brazilian concretism, or of Foucault's language of the exterior. Rather, it is the emptiness of the popular language of those in contemporary media who fictionalize reality as the *samsara* of ideology, subordinating everything and everyone to the logic of capital.

3

Refiguring the Poundian Ideogram

From Octavio Paz's "Blanco/ Branco" to Haroldo de Campos's *Galáxias*

MARJORIE PERLOFF

In March 1968, Octavio Paz, then residing in New Delhi as the Mexican ambassador to India, wrote to thank Haroldo de Campos in São Paulo for the manifestos and poems by the Noigandres group the latter had sent him. Paz was as intrigued by the concretists' theory of the "constellation"—a term derived from Stéphane Mallarmé's "Un coup de dés"—as he was skeptical about their devotion to Ezra Pound, and especially Pound's inclusion of actual Chinese ideograms in the *Cantos*. Paz's commentary is worth citing at some length:

> I understand that you [meaning the whole Noigandres group] see in Pound a precursor. I must point out, however, that Pound's poetry—fundamentally discursive—does not actually make use of ideograms, but rather *descriptions of ideograms*. . . . In certain passages of the *Cantos* [Pound introduces] real Chinese ideograms: they are cited in a foreign language that, to be understood, requires their translation into our discursive language. Our [Western] languages are the extreme opposite of Chinese, and the most that can be done is

> what you people (not Pound) are doing: to create plastic and syntactic procedures that, more than imitating ideograms, become their metaphor, their analogic double. . . . Mallarmé's case . . . is different from Pound's: there is no description, and discourse is reduced to its enunciation. Mallarmé sees the word as the center of semantic irradiations—which brings him closer to the ideogram—but none of his words is self-sufficient: the unity is the sentence that, in turn, generates discourse. The revolution of "Un coup de dés" (pardon my playing with words) is its rotation of sentences. . . . Mallarmé does not renounce discourse: he fragments it and, by confronting one fragment against the other, sets in motion the entire set. This is what he calls a *constellation*: signs in rotation [E o que ele chama *constelação*: signos em rotação].[1]

The distinction Paz makes here between Pound and Mallarmé is telling: for Paz, the introduction of *actual* Chinese ideograms—which is to say, alien elements—into the discourse of a given poem is problematic. In Paz's view, a poem, however fragmented, as is Mallarmé's "Un coup de dés," is necessarily *discursive*, and the discourse, a "rotation of sentences," cannot be interrupted by translation from one language into another. If, as Paz says of Mallarmé, the word is seen "as the center of semantic irradiations"—rich in meanings that radiate from its material form—then the "self-sufficient" word or ideogram is an intrusion.

A similar point had already been made by Paz in *The Bow and the Lyre* (*El arco y la lira* [1956; rev. and expanded, 1967]). "Pound," he declared, "accumulates quotations with the heroic air of one who robs graves" (Pound acumula las citas con un aire heroico de saqueador de tumbas). He "offers us so many and such diverse traditions because he himself has none," and thus the *Cantos* lack "a central tradition" (revelan . . . cierta falta de centro).[2] This critique becomes more pointed in a later essay, "¿Poesía latinoamericana?," in which Paz observes:

> The method of the *Cantos* is founded on a false analogy—what Pound called presentation is really little more than juxtaposition. . . . What do Chinese ideograms signify *inside* a text written in English? There are only two possibilities: the citations demand translation which isn't ideographic, or the ideograms are magic traces, signs that have lost the power to signify . . .
>
> [Pound's] theory is barbaric and arrogant. The barbarism and arrogance of the conquistador: Rome is no Babel.[3]

For the Noigandres poets, however, these were by no means the only two alternatives: the ideogram or "constellation" does in fact create new meanings by its visual placement on the page and its particular context. Then, too, Pound almost invariably gives us the English equivalent of a given ideogram a line or two after its appearance, so that the texture of the *Cantos*, or Canto-text, becomes bilingual. The goal is not to have ideogram X translated but to allow that ideogram to function in its relationships to neighboring words—and to its own English equivalent.

In the preface to "Un coup de dés," Mallarmé himself makes clear that the radical visual design of his great poem does not really oppose the discursive structure of the traditional poem. In the original French printing in *Cosmopolis* (1897), the opening words, "UN COUP DE DÉS," inevitably take the reader to "JAMAIS" at the bottom of the first page, then to "N'ABOLIRA" four pages later, and finally to "LE HASARD." In the author's note that introduced the poem in 1897, Mallarmé explains that "*the whole* [*is*] *without novelty* except for the way the reading process is spaced out. The 'blanks,' in effect, assume importance and are what is immediately most striking; versification always demanded them as a surrounding silence, so that a lyric poem . . . generally occupies about a third of the leaf on which it is centered: *I don't transgress against this order of things, I merely disperse its elements*."[4]

This dispersal of elements, emphasizing pause, hesitation, and silence—an alternate speeding up and slowing down of the discourse—is further complicated by the variations in typography that structure "Un coup de dés." But although, as Mallarmé tells us, "the Page . . . is taken as the basic unit, in the way that elsewhere the Verse or the perfect line is," we should note that the conventions of phrasal and clausal structure remain intact.[5] For example:

SI

La lucide et seigneuriale aigrette du vertige
au front invisible
scintille
puis ombrage
une stature mignonne ténébreuse debout
en sa torsion de sirène

[***IF***

The lucid and lordly crest of vertigo
invisible on the brow
scintillates
then shadows
a delicate dark form standing upright
in its Siren twist][6]

Here, the delicate suspension pattern initiated by the "*SI*" (*IF*) underscores the difficulty of the imagery: what is "the lucid and lordly crest of vertigo"? And whose the "delicate dark form / in its siren twist"? But the clauses are complete in ways antithetical to the movement of the later *Cantos*, such as Canto 77, with their shifts in tonal and linguistic registers.[7] In the scene set in the Pisan prison camp, the movement is from the Chinese ideogram for dawn (*tan*) to the slangy "sht house" and Southern drawl of "doin' nawthin' / not fishin', just watchin' the water," to the eloquent formal refrain, "Nothing counts save the quality of the affection," to a second ideogram *K'ou* (mouth), positioned next to the phrase "god's mouth," and then to gossip about the old Bohemian days in a London studio, and a reference to the intriguing Grishkin of T. S. Eliot's quatrain poem "Whispers of Immortality," his most sustained attempt at writing a twentieth-century English metaphysical poem.

Here, as Paz objected, Rome *is* Babel, although we do not, in fact, need to translate the ideograms into English, the neighboring words themselves providing the referent within the Poundian "periplum." Ideogram thus acts as repetition and as visual analogue rather than as a word to be translated. Notice how the dawn rises in the central portion of the page in the opening line, even as, further down, the sun-mouth is seen rising in the East. The technique is indeed, as Paz remarked critically, the juxtaposition and jostling of unlike elements.

Now let us turn to Paz's poem "Blanco," written in 1966 and published the following year. The author's headnote immediately strikes a more Mallarméan than Poundian note: "*Blanco*: white; blank; an unmarked space; emptiness, void; the white mark in the center of a target."[8] We are told that the poem "was meant to be read as a succession of signs on a single page"—a page that "unfolds vertically" like "a roll of Tantric pictures and emblems." One need not resort to Tantric analogies to make sense of the visual production of the poem since Paz, like the cosmopolitan modernists with whom he came into contact, was a world traveler and a tourist. Suffice it to add that the first printing of the poem consisted of a single sheet of paper folded in the manner of a street map or a set of accordion postcards. Nonetheless, in the headnote Paz insists further on the metaphysical dimension of the printing process: "[The] arrangement of temporal order is the form adopted by the course of the poem: its discourse corresponds to another which is spatial: the separate parts which comprise the poem are distributed like the sections, colors, symbols, and figures of a mandala."[9] The poem can be read, Paz explains, in four ways: as a whole or as three separate columns. The columns are, in turn, divided into eight, six, and eight poems respectively, each column organized by the number four: the four elements (left), four colors (yellow, red, green, blue; center), and four emotions (right).

This mandala charting suggests right away that the core of "Blanco" is thematic. Take, for example, the first instance of left–right columns, following the opening:

en el muro la sombra del fuego	*llama rodeada de leones*
en el fuego tu sombra y la mía	*leona en el circo de las llamas*
	ánima entre las sensaciones

el fuego te desata y te anuda
Pan Grial Ascua *frutos de luces de bengala*
Muchacha *los sentidos se abren*
tú ríes—desnuda *en la noche magnética*
en los jardines de la llama
La pasión de la brasa compasiva[10]

[on the wall the shadow of the fire *flame encircled by lions*
in the fire your shadow and mine *lioness in the circus of the flames*
soul among sensations

the fire unlaces and fastens you
Ember Bread Grail *fruits of the fireworks*
Girl *the senses open*
you laugh—naked *in the magnetic night*
in the gardens of the flame
The passion of compassionate coals][11]

Here the left column is an incantation to fire—the flames serving as backdrop for the image of the naked laughing girl of the poet's dreams—while the right column is a slight variation on this theme, presenting the beloved as lioness (*leona*) in the circle or circus of flames, "ánima entre las sensaciones." The sensations on the right correspond to the fire images on the left to create the erotic complex of *La pasión de la brasa compasiva* (the passion of compassionate coals), the line initiating a new center column, in which the fire imagery now gives way to the second element, water, "oleaje de sílabas húmedas."

Paz's elaborate sound structures—"La pasión de la brasa compasiva," for example—exploit both the internal rhyme of *pas/bras* and then its echo in *compasiva*. They underscore the lyric intensity of "Blanco," an intensity quite different from the mock-epic collage structure of Pound's *Cantos*, with their constant shift of tones and voices. Language / the female body / the natural world: these are orchestrated by Paz without the "interruption" of proper names, slang locutions, or particles from other languages: the poem proceeds from the stirring (*el comienzo*) of the beginning to the final *realidad a la Mirada*.[12]

Haroldo's "Branco" renders the original faithfully. Here is his translation of the two columns above:

no muro a sombra do fogo *chama rodeada de leões*
no fogo tua e minha sombras *leoa no círculo das chamas*
alma animando sensações

o fogo te ata e desata
Pão Graal Áscua *frutos de fogos-de-bengala*
Mulher *os sentidos se exabrem*

teu riso—nua *na noite magnética*
entre os jardins da chama
Paixão de brasa compassiva[13]

Haroldo's own poetics, very different from Octavio Paz's, manifests itself in *Galáxias* (1984), which translates straightforwardly into English and French as *Galaxies*, and in his theoretical writings of the period.[14] In his early writings—for example, the well-known essay "The Open Work of Art" (1955)—Haroldo's allegiance is still to "the Mallarméan constellation-poem" and its "concept of multi-divisions or capillary structure." "Silence," he writes, "emerges from that truly verbal rosette, 'Un coup de dés,' as the primordial element of rhythmic organization."[15] But even here, Haroldo recognizes that there are other paradigms, especially the Joycean one. To wit: "Mallarmé developed a visual notion of graphic space, served by the prismatic notation of poetic imagination in ebbs and flows which are dislocated like the elements of a mobile, utilizing silence in the way that Calder used air. Joyce, on the other hand, holds to the materialization of a 'poly-dimensional limitless flow'—the 'durée réelle,' the 'riverrun of 'élan vital'—which obliges him to undertake a true atomization of language, where each 'verbi-voco-visual' unit is at the same the continent-content of the whole work and instantly 'myriad minded.'"[16] In other words, Mallarméan graphic space has justly been received as a virtuoso representation of sound and silence, the "deep" images themselves retaining their complex semantic resonance. But Joyce tops this technique by atomizing the language itself, breaking down each unit into its multidimensional "verbi-voco-visual" components. Pound does it even more fully; his "Pisan Cantos," says Haroldo, "are organized by the ideogrammatic method, permitting a perpetual block of ideas which affect each other reciprocally."[17] And again, in a related essay, "the device of ideogrammatic montage invades the microstructure of the composition."[18]

Concrete poetry, Haroldo argued in this early period, replaces "richness of vocabulary" with "*richness of structure*," severely reducing the language field so as to avoid all excess and hence redundancy.[19] But with the turn in the 1970s to what he called the "baroquizing" of the earlier model, the writing of his own "barraucous ibericane mortalepic" called *Galáxias*, Haroldo was searching for new ways of renewing his own Brazilian tradition: "To write, today, in both Europe and Latin America will mean, more and more, to rewrite, to rechew. *Oi barbaroi*. The Vandals, long ago, crossed the borders and are crowding the senate and the agora. . . . Logocentric writers who imagined themselves the privileged beneficiaries of a proud one-way koine may now prepare themselves for the increasingly urgent task of acknowledging and redevouring the differential marrow of the new barbarians of the polytopic and polyphonic planetary civilization."[20] *The differential marrow*: whereas Paz's "Blanco" absorbed Eastern (primarily Tantric Indian) erotic elements into the fabric of his Western lyric meditation, Haroldo's *Galáxias* turns to polyglottism and ideogram. Nonetheless, as Haroldo makes clear in his remarkable *Ideograma*, what interests him the most is not "the 'pictographic' argument (the ideogram as a painting of ideas via things), but rather the 'relational' argument (the ideogram as a relational process, as a structural metaphor)."[21] How this works in practice is clarified in Haroldo's 1976 essay "The Ghost in the Text (Saussure and the Anagrams)," in which he discusses the anagrammatization of the name "Lygia" (in the poem "Lygia Fingers," by his writer sibling, Augusto de Campos): "[The name's] complete or partial phonemes [are] redistributed through other words (*digital*, *linx*, *felyna*, *figlia*, etc.), which themselves function as metonymic or metaphoric emblems of femininity and its attributes. Like the ancient Germanic poets, who used colored stones to mark the phonemes of their composition, the concrete poet made use of his own notation, in which different colors distinguish different reading 'parts' (in the musical sense)."[22] Note that this is a very different conception of concretism from that of the earlier Noigandres manifesto, with its emphasis on graphic space as structural agent and verbal-visual homology. Paragram, anaphone, hypogram: like the Saussure of the anagram studies, Haroldo came to conceive of the ideogram less as constellation than as a set of morphemes that generated possibilities for paragrammatic play. "Concrete poetry"—as Haroldo put it in his 1981 essay "Anthropophagous Reason," following Roman Jakobson—"rethought its own code, the poetic function itself . . . it became a question of assuming, critiquing, and 'chewing up' a poetics."[23]

In *Galáxias*, this process takes a decidedly unPazian—indeed, unMallarméan—turn. Haroldo's own headnote (not included in the original Portuguese-language edition of 1984) is telling:

> An audiovideotext, videotextogram, the *galáxias* situate themselves on the border between prose and poetry. In this kaleidoscopic book, there's an epic, narrative gesture . . . but the image remains, the vision or calling of the epiphanic. In that sense it is the poetic pole that ends up prevailing in the project, and the result is 50 "galactic cantos," with a total of more than 2000 lines (close to 40 per page). This permutational book has, as its semantic backbone, a recurrent yet always varied theme all along: travel as a book and the book as travel. . . . Two *formants*, in italics, the initial one (beginning-end: "and here I begin") and the final one (end-beginning-new beginning), encompass the game of moveable pages, interchangeable in their reading, where each isolated fragment introduces its "difference," but contains, in itself, like a watermark, the image of the entire book.[24]

This passage is fundamentally concerned with travel as book and the book as travel in a format of "moveable pages, *interchangeable* in their reading" (my emphasis). Such interchangeability is hardly characteristic of *Blanco*, which gradually builds to the crescendo of "Your body / spilled on my body" (Tu cuerpo / derramado en mi cuerpo).[25] Rather, Haroldo's "moveable pages" recall the paratactic structure, with its elaborate repetitions of Pound's *Cantos*. Consider the following "galactic" prose poem, the eighth of the *Galáxias* ("isto não é um livro," dated August 2, 1964), both in the original and in the French translation by Inês Oseki-Dépré and the author.[26]

"Isto não é um livro" is Haroldo's "livre de voyage" (livro de viagem), his "Baedeker d'epiphanies" (baedeker de epifanias) or "epiphanie en Baedeker" (epifania em baedeker). This composition turns its chosen genre—the voyage poem—inside out. For, rather than describing, in minute detail, a particular town in a particular country, this poem juxtaposes opposites: placid Switzerland, specifically Genève-Genf-Geneva (with a pun on *geneve*, juniper) and Zurich with its Zürichsee, in the heart of Europe, versus the exotic capital of the province of Paraíba in northeastern Brazil, called João Pessoa (which immediately evokes the name of the great Portuguese poet Fernando Pessoa). The city of João Pessoa is known for its violent street life and becomes the setting of the sordid tale of a signorina (sometimes fraülein), the little prostitute murdered in a one-night cheap hotel; but then again this Miss Stromboli may be an "entreteneuse entertainer," spotted in a Swiss café. Like film dissolves, the poem's narrative threads never cohere, nor does it matter whether this "poupette etranglée," the victim of the "peresdelapatrie" who are "chefs de l'industrie," is Swiss or Brazilian, for the poem's collage of newspaper headlines, tabloid tales, and travel-book descriptions of particular churches, locations, and violent actions suggests that the scene is the same everywhere, thus ironically echoing the opening quatrain in Baudelaire's "Le Voyage":

> Pour l'enfant, amoureux de cartes et d'estampes,
> L'univers est égal à son vaste appétit.
> Ah! que le monde est grand à la clarté des lampes!
> Aux yeux du souvenir que le monde est petit![27]

The light source, in Haroldo's voyage, is appropriately double edged: the *pluiesoleil* (rainsun) of summer, even though, according to legend, the sun rises first in João Pessoa. Contradiction is at the heart of the poem. In the course of his *Galáxias*, Haroldo uses heavy compounding and portmanteau words, the new words like *pourquoi pas* (*porquenão*) arranged in elaborate phrasing created by repetition, unpunctuated, and piled up into one long strophe with no full stops, no complete sentences. Like Pound, Haroldo has a predilection for multilingualism, shifting readily from English to German to Italian. The references can be to modernist literary topoi, like Faulkner's appropriation of a line from *Macbeth* for the title of *The Sound and the Fury*, as in the *galáxia*, which also paraphrases in Portuguese the opening line of Paul Valéry's *Le cimetière marin*.

Let me explain first that this "galaxy," as each individual poem is also called, is dated November 19, 1963 (dates and first lines identify shifts from one galaxy to another), and begins as well with a direct quotation from *Macbeth*: "multitudinous seas incarnadine." It then proceeds to propose an analogy between the foamy tide of the sea and the blank page of the book: "the sea and the froth and the foam the frothfoam of the sea begun always again and recommencing the time abolished in the heterogeneous green" (o mar mas a escuma mas a espuma mas a espumaescuma do mar recomeçado e recomeçando o tempo abolido no verde vário). This recommencing of time actively resists linearity because it is conveyed poetically through the implementation of many forms of sonic and rhythmic repetition: alliteration, internal anaphora, copulative parataxis, chiasmus, and so forth. The combination of citations and rhetorical figures reaches a climax toward the end of the page (each galaxy takes up one unnumbered page and consists of forty-two to forty-six lines innocent of punctuation or the use of uppercase): "the gargoylesque and gargling sea, that garrulously warbling sea that book sea that marked sea book/variegatedly faded and florally multitudinous sea incarnadine" (o mar gárgulo e gargáreo/gorjeando gárrulo esse mar esse mar livro esse livro mar marcado/vário murchado e flóreo multitudinoso mar purpúreo).

Whereas Pound's references are usually stubbornly literal and documentary, as they are to a degree in the galaxy just quoted, elsewhere Haroldo's baroque spin on the *Cantos* lets the fantastic and bizarre dominate. The following passage is from the galaxy that begins with the Magritte-like statement, "this is not a book"—"isto não é um livro" (dated August 2, 1964):

> naquele dia
> em genève abrindo genf manchetes nos jornais miss stromboli explodindo
> como um geyser dos cabelos ruivos estrangulamento porcerto e a
> esfaqueada pequena pobre prostituta paraibana de morenos pentefinos
> pentelhos sem nom de guerre sangrando na morte cheirando urina . . .
> ce jour-là
> à génève ouvrant genf manchettes dans les journaux miss stromboli explosant
> comme un geyser aux cheveux roux étranglement poursûr et la
> poignardée petite pauvre prostitutée paraïbanaise aux bruns peignefins
> poils pubiens sans nom de guerre saignant dans la mort sentant l'urine . . .[28]

What gives Haroldo's "prose" its particular charge is the combination of collage cut, as in "à Genève ouvrant genf manchettes," where the city name is inserted in German between the verb and its object, or in the abrupt shift into English in "miss Stromboli," with obsessive verbal and sound repetition, whether rhyme, alliteration, assonance, and anaphora, as in "poignardée petite pauvre prostituée paribanaise au bruns peignefins," or "peignefins poils pubiens."

At the same time, visual patterns are created by linking nonadjacent words as in *sangrando/cheriando* (saignant/sentant), and thus setting up the deflationary introduction of urine at the end of the line. The last two lines of the *galáxia* that begins with the words "isto não é um livro" are especially effective in this regard:

gordos paisdapátria pupeta estrangulda sem saber como saber quem saberia
que sua sorte sua morte seu porte minúsculo vulcão de matéria narrada
gras pèresdelapatrie poupette étranglée sans savoir comment savoir qui saurait
que son sort sa mort son port minuscule volcan de matière narrée

Here the irony is that the *paisdapátria*—those sinister fathers of their country who are also Brazil's *chefetes de indústria*—are linked by sound to the very *pupeta estranguida* who is their victim. Language creates strange bedfellows. And the *paisdapátria pupeta* ideogram is followed by the intricate variations on *saber* (to know)—*sem saber como saber quem saberia*. Who indeed will have known what really happened to this miniscule volcano named Miss Stromboli? The chanting rhythm of *sua sorte sua morte seu porte* (*son sort sa mort son port*) leaves the "narrated matter" (*matéria narrada*) unresolved. Highly consonant as the words are on the microlevel, they never attain any sort of closure.

Unlike "Branco"—Haroldo's translation of Paz's "Blanco"—*Galáxias* can be seen as an experiment with what Haroldo himself called "the differential marrow." Constellation, in the Mallarméan form of the self-contained poem, gives way to a sequence of ideograms, where words like "stromboli" and "geneve" become ciphers—what Paz called "magic traces," untranslatable into a discursive equivalent. In the final section of "Blanco," we read the climactic lines:

la transparencia es todo lo que queda	transparency is all that remains
Tus pasos en el cuarto vecino	Your footsteps in the next room
el trueno verde	the green thunder
madura	ripening
en el follaje del cielo	in the foliage of the sky
Estás desnuda	You are naked
como una sílaba	like a syllable[29]

But for the Haroldo of *Galáxias*, there is no transparency and certainly no homology between landscape and the nude female body or between that body and the poetic Word, as happens in Paz. His syllables are "naked" only to the extent that they have been removed from their verbal-morphemic matrix.

Consider the role, once again in Haroldo's second *voyage* poem (the *galáxia* dated August 2, 1964), of the reference to a wind burning "quando um cisne morre no zürichsee" (in the French translation, "quand un cygne meurt dans la zürichsee"). One thinks immediately of those great swans of French *symboliste* poetry: Baudelaire's, which, having escaped from its cage, moves awkwardly along the Paris pavement, and Mallarmé's superb but helpless "cygne d'autrefois," trapped in the frozen lake. But Haroldo's swan, dying in the *Zürichersee*, is just grist for the newspaper mill in a Switzerland where *nada* seems to be happening "in the day-years of the days composed of year-weeks" (nos anosdias dos dias de semanas-anos).

Then, too, as has been suggested by José María Rodríguez García, Haroldo's *cisne* may well be a playful allusion to Paz's *Le singe grammairien*, a book-length prose poem, an Indian travelogue, and an exercise in *écriture du corps*, which he chose to publish first in French, where the wordplay on *cygne/singe* would be remarked on. Publication of the Spanish original, *El mono gramático* (*The Monkey Grammarian*), was deferred until 1974.[30] In the closely intertwined vignettes and monologues that compose this Tantric poem, writing is always related to the sex act. The woman who excites the writing is a Janus-faced persona; she is divided into two separate key female figures, both named "Esplendor," one Eastern, one Western. Women are ubiquitous in Paz's eroticized texts, but, unlike Esplendor, they are also always silent. Esplendor comes to represent a blank sheet of paper on which the poet inscribes his phallic power. She is allowed to speak because she embodies the signifying potentiality of the blank page, which in turn excites a late ethnographic-surrealist poet known for eroticizing writing and equating sexual climax with both an epiphany and a mystical rapture. Surrealist wordplay, pun, anagram, however dazzling their virtuosity, cannot make up for what Rodríguez García, who has studied *El mono gramático* carefully, characterizes as its problematic phallocentrism, its radical dismemberment throughout of the textual/female body.[31] Paz's fondness for ecstatic exclamation is carried to its extreme in the last section of "Blanco": "the world / is the cleft the splendor the whirl" (el mundo / es la grieta el resplandor el remolino).[32]

Galáxias avoids such equations; its own structure of repetitions and syntactic ambiguity emphasizes difference rather than identity. In Haroldo's world, the *event*—here the coming together of man and woman in a mystic union—no longer carries conviction; it is absorbed into the larger textual field. Like the swan, the little *prostituta paribanaisa* becomes a link in a larger verbal/sonoric chain. Juxtaposition of ideographic notations thus replaces the surreal metaphoric intensity of Paz's lyric. Not the *white* and *silence* of "Blanco/Branco" but the nightmare of everyday life.

4

Poetry Makes Nothing Happen

MARÍLIA LIBRANDI

I have chosen this textual encounter through translation between Octavio Paz and Haroldo de Campos to propose a comparatist analysis of their work, focusing on the transparent image that synthesizes and approximates their poetical project. This image is condensed in the titles *Blanco/Transblanco*,[1] and it establishes a bridge between their Luso-Hispanic poetic project and the field of world literature. My intention is to show that transparency is also the image (or absence of image) that both poets use in their defense of poetry and of its healing effects against the nightmares of history.

To address the politics of Paz's and Campos's poetics through an analysis of the image of transparency, I compare the presence of blank spaces in *Blanco/Transblanco* (read here as a Luso-Hispanic unit) with the one that appears in *Galáxias*, a collection of fifty texts written by Haroldo de Campos from 1963 to 1976. If in "Blanco," Paz melted the French vanguardist tradition with a Buddhist erotic philosophy based on a meditation of the mandala to attain *sunyata* (the supreme state of being in nothingness), in *Galáxias*, Campos creates a "kaleidoscopic book," the aim of which is to produce epiphanic moments with words "carrying a mantric, 'transmental,' value."[2] "Blanco" and *Galáxias* are also close to one another as "travel books," written as the result of a journey: in Campos's case, to fifty distinct places, and in Paz's case, to India.

In sum, my own text has a specific target (*blanco*): to understand the presence and the praise of transparency as a blank space in the texts of Haroldo de Campos and Octavio Paz. To do this, I focus on one page from *Galáxias*, its second fragment that refers to the city of Granada, Spain (which Campos visited in 1959), and that starts with the proverb "reza, calla y trabaja" (pray, be silent and work) in conjunction with a reading of the poem "Blanco" by Octavio Paz. Both works are texts written as a result of a displacement: to Granada, in the case of Haroldo de Campos, a city that can be considered an Eastern land (the Orient) within the Iberian Peninsula, with its Arab and Jewish presence and influence until the fifteenth century; and to India, in Octavio Paz's case. My focal question is, Why is transparency the center of these texts that here I am calling "blank poems"?

The first reference that unites these texts is Stephane Mallarmé and his explicit defense in the preface to "Un coup de dés" (A throw of the dice) of a poetic rhythm no longer measured by meter or by rhyme but by blank spaces: "Les 'blancs' en effet, assument l'importance, frappent d'abord; la versification en exigea, comme silence alentour" (The "blanks," in effect, assume importance and are what is immediately most striking; versification always demanded them as a surrounding silence).[3] With Mallarmé, blank space became part of a new space that the poem begins to inhabit on the page with letters acting as *punti luminosi*, like stars in a constellation in the formal structure of the poem. One of the epigraphs of "Blanco" is Mallarmé's verse: "Avec ce seul objet dont le Néant s'honore" (With this sole object that Nothingness attains).[4] In *Galáxias*, Haroldo de Campos also includes an epigraph from Mallarmé: "La fiction affleurera et se dissipera, vite, d'après la mobilité de l'écrit" (The fiction rises to the surface and quickly dissipates, following the variable motion of the writing).[5] In the former, *le Néant* has both a noble association (with honor) and a sonorous one (*s'honore*), referring to the most noble of all sounds: silence. In the case of Campos's epigraph, the blank is part of a movement of appearing and disappearing that transforms what would be an epic text (relating to travel) into an epiphanic one. This presence of Mallarmé could explain the source of the blanks in these texts, but it does not yet answer the question of why transparency becomes the poem's dominant goal, not just part of its formal composition but also its target.

The answer I propose is twofold. I first suggest that, in these texts, "blanco" is the color of mourning. In this sense, I propose reading these texts as elegies, as funereal texts. If this suggestion is correct, then who are the dead that are being honored? Poetry itself, probably, and its presence as "the art of disappearance" (to follow Baudrillard)[6] or as "rien ou presque un art" (nothing or perhaps what merely verges on art) as Mallarmé has it.[7] In parallel with this sense of negation, obliteration, and death, "blanco" (or, better, transparency) also acts as a celebration of poetry and of something else (transcendent) given a positive value: nirvana, Eden, that which appears in each one of these poets in different ways. "Blanco" in Paz appears as an origin and end of the poem with a mystic and utopian role. In Campos, it appears as the middle and the medium, as an incorporation of other texts and authors in his poems: Dante, Guido Cavalcanti, and Ezra Pound, specifically related to the presence of white in issues of translation. White in Campos is also linked to Goethe's idea of universal literature, where the color is understood as the result of the union of all colors. I propose that we should have two sorts of "blanco." At the negative end of the spectrum, "blanco" is related to death. At the positive end, "blanco" is linked to life in a state of plenitude produced by a text in pilgrimage to heaven. It is a voyage to "an East to the East of the East" (um Oriente ao Oriente do Oriente) as Álvaro de Campos/Fernando Pessoa puts it.[8]

Via Auden

Why is transparency a target for Paz and Campos? To begin to answer this question, I develop a mediated comparative analysis of *Blanco/Transblanco* and *Galáxias* through a reading of W. H. Auden's poem "In Memory of W.B. Yeats."[9] As in Auden's elegy, we find in "Blanco" an elegy to "México *caído*," to fallen Mexico, and in *Galáxias*'s second fragment, an elegy to Federico García Lorca's assassination and the consequences of the Spanish Civil War.

As soon as he disembarked in New York City in January 1939, Auden received word of the death of William Butler Yeats. He wrote "In Memory of W.B. Yeats" as an elegy in praise of the poet and a defense of poetry in times of war. This defense becomes even stronger, because he praises poetry as a source of healing and, at the same time, points out its failure, its inability to alter the brutal course of world events. The verse that synthesizes this ambivalence is "Poetry makes nothing happen," considered by Joseph Brodsky to be "the statement of an era."[10] In my reading, Paz's and Campos's texts could be read as reverberations of the same issue that disturbed Auden: the conflicted relationship between poetry and history in the twentieth century. For this reason, and although Paz and Campos do not explicitly cite Auden, his poem is fundamental if we wish to understand the ambivalence that blank space attains in their poems: as I have said before, at the same time, "blanco" is present as the color of mourning (this results from historical wounds) and as the color of survival and of transcendence hidden by its transparency.

The elegy is composed of three parts. There are three points from Auden's poem that are worth highlighting here, each related to one of its parts. The first is the presence of white in the opening part of the poem as wintertime, as frozen landscape and snow:

I
He disappeared in the dead of winter:
The brooks were frozen, the airports almost deserted,
And snow disfigured the public statues;
The mercury sank in the mouth of the dying day.
What instruments we have agree
The day of his death was a dark cold day.

Then, in the second part of the poem, the poet addresses Yeats directly:

II
You were silly like us; your gift survived it all:
The parish of rich women, physical decay,
Yourself. Mad Ireland hurt you into poetry.
Now Ireland has her madness and her weather still,
For poetry makes nothing happen: it survives
. . .
. . . it survives,
A way of happening, a mouth.

Auden presents the concomitant power and failure of poetry as an unresolved tension, the same tension that one finds re-enacted in Paz's and Campos's texts. This dilemma is what occurs between the donation of a poem (as a sort of gift), which keeps language alive and through which truth shows itself, and its failure. As Brodsky commented on Auden: "I realized that I was reading a poet who spoke the truth—or through whom the truth made itself audible."[11] But then there is also the failure of the poem to prevent pain, war, and misery. "Poetry makes nothing happen" refers to poetry's powerlessness in the face of difficult questions; and more prosaically, it is not considered an action in the world of stock market transactions (which Auden's verses make clear when he juxtaposes the death of Yeats to the noise of the era, "When the brokers are roaring like beasts on the floor of the Bourse"). Thus, "poetry makes nothing happen" expresses poetry's failure, but it also expresses its maximum power. To make nothing happen is an attribute of God's creation that started from nothing: "Light! And light was made." In this sense, "poetry makes nothing happen" is an ambivalent verse just as the presence of transparency—another way to say "nothing"—is in Campos and Paz. In them, this modern dilemma seems to be resolved or synthesized in whiteness and blank space, an image of absence in poetry and its maximum presence as light, as "heavenly trans-illumination," in Campos's words.

In the last stanza, Auden asks the earth to receive Yeats's body: "Earth, / receive an honoured guest: / William Yeats is laid to rest." Meanwhile his voice remains and brings us joy amid the sadness of the times, about which Auden writes: "With your unconstraining voice / Still persuade us to rejoice." Most importantly, the poet teaches us to praise, and this teaching liberates us from the pain and imprisonment of modernity: "In the deserts of the heart / Let the healing fountain start, / In the prison of his days / Teach the free man how to praise." Poems teach us "how to praise"—for they sing our failure and our death—and we find something similar in the poems of Campos and Paz: they were created as songs of healing.

Haroldo de Campos: *Galáxias*

In the prose poem *Galáxias*,[12] the narration is constantly interrupted, never finished, and left in suspense; facts appear and disappear, and the reader must play the role of detective. Historical elements appear in a state of latency, presented or hidden by omnipresent transparency; *Galáxias* is a text invented as a palimpsest in which the written text is erased so that more can be written over it, only to be erased, and so on. The sequence that interests me here takes place during the poet's travel to Granada, in 1959, in the Plaza San Nicolás, located in the Albaicín district. It corresponds to the second page, or second "galactic chant" (according to the author's definition). One immediately observes two elements of time: Franco era and Catholic Spain, on the one hand, and the absent presence of Muslim al-Andalus from the eighth through the sixteenth centuries, on the other.[13]

The "chant" begins with a proverb, "reza calla y trabaja" (pray, be silent and work). Campos then alters this initial verse by way of a repetition that serves to transform its base ideology. *Rezar*—to pray—is transformed into the poem text's own rhythm, like a mantra. As in Auden, this poem also teaches us "how to pray"; *calla* is the uninterrupted silence, perturbed by historic events, and is transformed into the white "cal" (limestone) of the walls; *trabaja* is the incessant movement of the text itself, always incorporating, mixing, advancing, or retreating without end. Right at the beginning, one finds all these elements in condensed form:

> Reza calla y trabaja em um muro de granada trabaja y calla y reza y calla y trabaja y reza em granada um muro da casa del chapiz ningún holgazán ganará el cielo olhando para baixo um muro interno la educación es obra de todos ave maria em granada mirad en su granada
>
> reza calla y trabaja on a wall in granada work in silence and pray and silence and work and pray in granada a wall at the moorish casa del chapiz no lazy bum will go to heaven seeing from above an inner wall la educación is the work of all ave maria in granada see him en su granada

In this opening segment, we see the proverb and its variations come together ("moorish casa del Chapiz") with expressions from the Franco era ("no lazy bum will go to heaven" or "education is the work of all") and Catholicism ("ave maria"). Finally, there is the very subtle remission to the verse of an elegiac poem, a poem written by Antonio Machado a few months after the assassination of Lorca: "en su granada."

Antonio Machado wrote his poem "El crimen fue en Granada" (The crime was in Granada) in October 1936 for Lorca, who was killed in August of that year.[14] Like Auden's poem, it is an elegy in three parts: the crime, the poet and his death, and the burial.

> Se le vio, caminando entre fusiles,
> por una calle larga,
> salir al campo frío,
> aún con estrellas, de la madrugada.
> Mataron a Federico
> cuando la luz asomaba.
>
> El pelotón de verdugos
> no osó mirarle la cara.
> Todos cerraron los ojos;
> rezaron: ¡ni Dios te salva!
> Muerto cayó Federico
> —sangre en la frente y plomo en las entrañas—
> . . . Que fue en Granada el crimen
> sabed—¡pobre Granada!—, en su Granada . . .
>
> [He was seen walking between rifles
> Down a long street
> And going out to the cold countryside
> Still with stars of early dawn.
> They killed Federico
> When light came.
> The squad of executioners
> Didn't dare look him in the face.
> They all closed their eyes.
> They prayed, "Not God can save you!"
> Dead fell Federico,
> —Blood on his forehead and lead in his stomach—.
> That crime was in Granada—
> —Know it—poor Granada!—in his Granada.]

In the second part, we see Lorca speaking with Death:

> "Hoy como ayer, gitana, muerte mía,
> qué bien contigo a solas,
> por estes aires de Granada, ¡mi Granada!"
>
> [Today as yesterday, gypsy, my death,
> how good alone with you
> in these breezes of Granada, my Granada!]

And then in the third part, we see his departure and burial:

> Se le vio caminar . . .
> Labrad, amigos,
> de piedra y sueño, en la Alhambra,
> un túmulo al poeta,
> sobre una fuente donde llore el agua,
> Y eternamente diga:
> el crimen fue en Granada, ¡en su Granada!
>
> [He was seen walking . . .
>   Friends, carve
> a tomb of stone and dream in the Alhambra,
> for the poet,
> over a fountain where the water weeps
> and forever says,
> The crime was in Granada, in his Granada!]

The fact that Lorca's death in Granada appears in Campos's text via this passage, via this particular fragment of verse, is indicative of its process of disappearing and appearing—like an iceberg, through which we see only the tip (in this case the very end of Machado's verse) as a clue left for the reader. Back with *Galáxias*, shortly after Campos's reference to "en su granada," we see the infinite presence of white:

> e depois a plazuela san nicolás o branco do branco do branco y calla no branco no branco no branco a cal um enxame de branco o branco . . .
>
> [and later plazuela san nicolas the white on white on white and silence in the white on white on white whitewash swarming white on white . . .]

Suddenly, white is interrupted by an event: "carros parando los guardias civiles o embaixador inglês fazendo turismo entre as galas do caudillo" (cars stopping the civil police the British ambassador sightseeing among caudillo's galas). The white presence is disturbed:

> e o branco violado a medula do branco ferida a fúria a alvúria do branco refluída sobre si mesma . . . rompido o sigilo do branco arisco árido do cálcio branco da cal que calla y trabaja . . . nunca mais a calma cal a calma cal calada do primeiro momento do primeiro branco
>
> [the violated white the marrow of white wounded the wrath of whiteness flowing over . . . broken the secrecy of white wild waterless white of whitewash that whispers and works . . . forever never but whispers and whitewash quiet whisper of the first white]

This violated "first white" is like what appears in Octavio Paz's work. "Blanco" in Paz is not peaceful; it is a result of anger, the same anger that appears in a poem he wrote in memory of the massacre of Tlatelolco, after Mexican troops killed student demonstrators shortly before the Olympic Games of 1968. Paz, in protest, resigned his post as Mexican ambassador to India and wrote this poem, later titled "Intermitencias del Oeste" (Interruptions from the West)[15]:

> La limpidez
> (quizá valga la pena
> escribirlo sobre la limpieza
> de esta hoja)
> no es limpida:
> es una rabia
> (amarilla y negra
> acumulacion de bilis en espanol)
> extendida sobre la pagina.
> Por que?
> *La vergüensa es ira*
> *vuelta contra uno mismo:*
> *si*
> *una nacion entera se averguenza*
> *es leon que se agazapa*
> *para saltar.*
> (Los empleados
> municipales lavan la sangre
> en la Plaza de los Sacrificios.)
> Mira ahora,
> manchada
> antes de haber dicho algo

que valga la pena,
la limpidez.
[Lucidity
(perhaps it's worth
writing across the purity
of this page)
is not lucid:
it is fury
(yellow and black
mass of bile in Spanish)
spreading over the page.
Why?
Guilt is anger
turned against itself:
if
an entire nation is ashamed
it is a lion poised
to leap.
(The municipal
employees wash the blood
from the Plaza of the Sacrificed.)
Look now,
stained
before anything worth it
was said:
lucidity.]

"Limpidez," here translated as "lucidity," also means transparency. "Lucidity . . . is not lucid: it is fury." This verse confirms the suspicion that this "blanco" is not peace but is rather the result of anger, as poetic expression in times of war and dictatorships.

To go back to the end of Campos's text, we see the relation between the blank space and the act of writing:

> agora escrevo agora a visão é papel e tinta sobre o papel o branco é papel yeserías atauriques y mocárabes de papel não devolvem senão a cutícula do tempo a lúnula da unha do tempo e por isso escrevo e por isso escravo roo a unha do tempo até o sabugo até o refugo até o sugo e não revogo a pátina de papel a pevide de papel a cáscara de papel a cortiça de papel que envolve o coração carnado de granada onde um vulcão sentados sobre explode e por isso calla y por eso trabaja y por eso

> [I write now the vision is paper and ink on paper the white is paper autauric stuccos and mozarab masses of paper do not return but the cuticle of time the lunule of the nail of time and that's why i write and that's why i'm a scribe on the nail of time gnawing down to the root of the nail root of the tail the juice of the junk i don't revoke the patina of paper the peel of paper the core of paper the paper cork that covers the crimson carnal heart of granada where a volcano sitting above explodes and that's why it whispers y por eso trabaja and that's why por eso]

His text is like ink on paper, rather like "yeserías atauriques" (autauric stuccos) that do not erase time but rather include time in its architecture, in its writing of text.

In *Galáxias*, we have a co-presence of temporal layers: present and absent al-Andalus and Spain in 1959, as well as the results of the Civil War, which began in 1936. We also have the reliance on the elegiac poem, and we have "blanco" that erases what it narrates, that imposes itself onto what is narrated and its time, and the perpetual movement of the text that never starts or finishes but is continuous. It defeats and overcomes historical times and its eras: the poem survives.

Octavio Paz: "Blanco"

Here, it is worthwhile to remember some of Octavio Paz's reflections on time and poetry. He described the relationship between poems and history (or time) as contradictory or even paradoxical: a poem is the fruit of a historic moment that it incorporates, but it can only be a great poem if it transcends and overtakes the historic moment that gave rise to it. Thus, the relationship is inverted: the poem forms the foundation of a society's history; it is its ontological groundwork. From there, Paz develops another correlated paradox concerning time: if the historic moment is dated, from which point the past is established, then the time of a poem is always the present as a timeless present, an archetypal time, he says. If the *Iliad* and the *Odyssey* could only have emerged in what we know as Greek society, each time we read these poems today we make present this past moment; the poem floats in time, says Paz. Auden has another way of saying it: it survives.

For Paz, the poem achieves a "consecration of the moment" (the instant consecration) by making present what we read. Campos argues something similar, in a text in which he seeks to define "poesia concreta": "Uma arte—não que apresente—mas que presentifique" (an art that does not present, but "presentifies" [makes present]).

In a 1978 letter to Paz, when the book proposal for *Transblanco* was confirmed, Campos said he would send Paz the book with his translation of Dante's six songs of *Paradise*, and the introductory essay "Luz: a escrita paradisiacal"

("Light: Paradisiacal Writing"). In this text, he cites the transcreation that Pound makes of Guido Cavalcanti through whiteness and blank spaces. This heavenly presence is a good measure of what Paz achieves in "Blanco." Paz's poem begins before the word is born, in a state of latency, and it moves toward the birth of its first creation: a flower.

un girasol
ya luz carbonizada
sobre un vaso
de sombra.
En la palma de una mano
ficticia,
flor
ni vista ni pensada:
oída,
aparece
amarillo
cáliz de consonantes y vocales
incendiadas
[a sunflower
light charred
in a vase
of shadow.
In the palm of an
invented hand,
the flower,
not seen nor imagined:
heard,
appears,
a yellow chalice
of consonants and vowels,
burning]

This flower is a flower of speech ("l'absente de tout bouquet"): I say flower—and a flower appears. But this heavenly movement has its limit in the river of blood that underlies it:

Patience patience
(Livingston en la sequía)
River rising a little
El mío es rojo y se agosta
Entre sableras llameantes:

Castillas de arena, naipes rotos
Y el jeroglífico (agua y brasa)
En el pecho del México caído.
Polvo soy de aquellos lodos.
Río de sangre,
                              Río de historias
De sangre,
              Río seco:
Boca de manantial
Amordazado
Por la conjuración anónima
De los huesos,
Por la ceñuda peña de los siglos
Y los minutos:
                              El lenguaje
Es una expiación,
                                   Propiciación
Al que no habla,
                              Emparedado
Cada día
              Asesinado,
El muerto innumerable.

[*Patience patience*
(Livingston in the drought)
River rising a little
Mine is red and scorches
in the flaming dunes:
Castiles of sand,
shredded playing cards,
and the hieroglyph (water and ember)
dropped on the chest of Mexico.
I am the dust of that silt
River of blood,
                              river of histories
of blood,
              dry river:
mouth of the source
gagged
by the anonymous conspiracy
of bones,
by the grim rocks of centuries

and minutes:
                    language
is atonement,
                    an appeasement
of the speechless,
                    the entombed,
the daily
          assassinated,
the countless dead.]

As in Auden's elegy, we find in "Blanco" an elegy to "Mexico caído" and to the results of the conquest. Paz's poetry comes from the same river of blood that served as the source for his "Blanco" poem—as "an appeasement / of the speechless, / the entombed, / the daily / assassinated, the countless dead." Then, in one of the most beautiful passages of "Blanco":

                    Hablar
Mientras los otros trabajan
Es pulir huesos,
                    Aguzar
Silencios
               Hasta la trasparencia,
Hasta la ondulación,
                    El cabrilleo,
Hasta el agua:

                    [To speak
while others work
is to polish bones,
                    sharpen
silence
               to transparency,
waves,
                    whitecaps
water]

Here is transparency again, expressed through an image of bones together with death. The final reference to water likewise reminds one of the Keats verse that serves as an inscription on his own tombstone: "Here lies one whose name was writ on water."

With these passages in mind, and by way of a conclusion, I would say this transparency re-establishes the *topos* of the Americas as a new world—that is, as a blank page on which to write, as a land to be peopled, and as a feminine body to be conquered. "Blanco" is contemporary with Paz's study of Claude Lévi-Strauss, which permits an anthropological reading of the text while bearing in mind Paz's role as an ambassador in India and his deep knowledge of the indigenous culture of Mexico. The blank spaces define his work, invoking what we find, for example, in the priest Manuel da Nóbrega's letter from 1549: "Acá pocas letras bastan, porque es todo papel blanco y no ay más que escrivir a plazer" (Here few letters are enough, because it is all white paper and we only need to write on it).[16]

Based on such colonial notions, as well as on the "blanco" that appears in the poems I have just examined, I wish to close with some correlations that may—in their excess and extremity—clarify something about the presence of transparency and of blank spaces in the work of Paz and in Campos. I would say that both "Blanco" and *Galáxias* are text voyages of non-conquerors, or rather, something like chronicles of inverted conquest. As conquerors, Paz and Campos come not to write but rather to erase what has been written and open a new space.

In this new space (once called the West Indies) that these texts offer us as a gift, I propose a final path to understand the presence of transparency. In a series of conversations with Bruce Albert, the Yanomami shaman Davi Kopenawa transmits to him his aspects of his community's philosophy.[17] As a shaman, Kopenawa is capable of seeing invisible spirits called *xapiripe*, which are transparent, iridescent emanations, mirrors that do not reflect but instead multiply light. The works of Paz and Campos, and particularly these poems, are similar to these mirrors that do not reflect but instead multiply light. According to Kopenawa, white people use strokes on paper so as not to forget. I would say that Paz and Campos (as poets of the Americas) write in order to forget, to erase historical pain, in order to show something else (whether called *xapiripe*, *sunyata*, or Eden), something that we do not see but that is here, hidden by its transparency.

5

Haroldo de Campos, Octavio Paz, and the Experience of the Avant-Garde

ANTONIO CICERO

No doubt one of the most striking of Haroldo de Campos's essays is "Poetry and Modernity: From the Death of Art to the Constellation. The Post-Utopian Poem," which was originally a lecture delivered in 1984 in the Instituto Nacional de Bellas Artes, in Mexico City, in a homage to Octavio Paz's seventieth birthday.[1] "Poetry and Modernity" is also the title of an important essay—originally a lecture delivered in 1989 at the University of Utah—by Octavio Paz.[2]

Taking these essays as points of departure, it is also about poetry and modernity that I would like to expound in what follows. At the end of his "Poetry and Modernity," Haroldo de Campos says, "I agree with Octavio Paz when he explains, in the final pages of *Children of the Mire*, that the poetry of our days is a poetry of the 'now' (although I prefer the expression 'nowness/Jetztzeit', which was dear to Walter Benjamin): that is, a poetry of 'the other present' and of 'plural history', which implies a 'critique of the future' and of its systematic paradises."[3] Confirming what he had said in *Children of the Mire*, Paz, in his own "Poetry and Modernity," explains that "for the ancients the past was the golden age, the natural Eden that we lost one day; for the moderns, the future was the chosen place, the promised land. But it is the present that has always been the time of poets and lovers, Epicureans and certain mystics. . . . Men and women will soon have to construct a morality, a politics, an erotics, and a poetics of present time."[4]

For Haroldo de Campos, such a poetry would be a "post-utopian" one. "Turned toward the future," he said, "the principle of hope is superseded by the principle of reality, whose foundation is anchored in the present."[5] According to him, avant-garde movements would not have been possible without what Ernst Bloch had called the Principle of Hope (das Prinzip Hoffnung), a principle indissoluble from the utopian perspective.[6] Striving after totalization, it favored utopian identity over individual singularities. Indeed, why would an artist deprived of the perspective of utopia renounce his individuality in the name of the anonymous teamwork of a particular movement? "Without the utopian perspective," he concluded, "the avant-garde movement loses its sense. . . . The totalizing project of the avant-garde, which ultimately could only be sustained by a redeeming utopia, is succeeded by the opening of a plurality of possible poetics."[7]

The wane of the utopian perspective—hence of the avant-garde movements—was explained by Haroldo de Campos as a consequence of the crisis of ideologies that resulted from the division of the world between, on the one hand, imperialist, savage, and predatory capitalism and, on the other hand, bureaucratic, repressive, and uniformizing states that, in their endeavor to convert artists into vassals of party dogmata, had no scruples in waving utopian banners. According to him, this is basically what explains the dissipation of the spell of utopia.

At this point I must confess that, although I agree that in the place of mutually excluding avant-garde movements we are now witnessing the development of a plurality of poetics, I do not feel at ease with Haroldo de Campos's attempt to explain this fact. While not denying the utopian component of most avant-garde movements, I do deny that their utopian perspectives are in all, or even in most, cases identified with political causes. In fact, it seems to me that, excepting some movements, such as different versions of futurism and a few versions of constructivism, this is simply not the case. Thus, expressionist, cubist, dada, and surrealist artists, for instance, are not necessarily involved with particular political creeds. In most cases, avant-garde artists and movements are committed to purely aesthetic or artistic utopias. This is why I do not think the failure of political utopias can account for the end of the avant-garde. We must look elsewhere for the explanation of this phenomenon.

In fact, I believe that the explanation for the end of the avant-garde does not lie in any extraneous factor but is the result of its consummation.[8] This is what I shall try to show in what follows.

At one point of his "Poetry and Modernity," Haroldo observes approvingly that in the eighteenth century, according to the German literary critic Hans

Robert Jauss, "the new element in the conception of what is modern lies in the introduction of the dimension of the future, in the utopian perspective. Instead of attributing to the past the ideal value of perfection, enlightened 'Modernity' wants to be judged by the increasingly critical view of a more and more advanced humanity."[9] In a similar vein, Paz, in his "Poetry and Modernity," asserts that "utopia is the other face of criticism, and only a critical age could be the inventor of utopias."[10] Modernity was certainly, as Kant had stated in the eighteenth century, "a critical age."[11] It began, as Paz remarks, "as a critique of religion, philosophy, morality, law, history, economics and politics. Criticism was its most distinctive feature, its birthmark. All that has been the modern age has been the work of criticism, which I take to mean a method of investigation, creation, and action. The principal concepts and ideas of the modern age—progress, evolution, revolution, freedom, democracy, science, technology—were born from that criticism."[12]

And, of course, modern criticism, far from sparing poetry, literature, or art, has been particularly active in these fields. To criticize means originally to distinguish, to separate, to classify, to compare. The rediscovery of ancient Roman poetry and its comparison to medieval Latin poetry was fatal to the latter. At the same time, possibilities inherent to the modern languages were brilliantly explored by the Provençal and the Italian poets. The contrast between ancient, medieval, and contemporary forms made some poets and critics begin to realize the relative—and therefore contingent—nature of inherited poetic forms. This was the beginning of a process during which, in the course of a few centuries, poets and critics became aware that poetry is one thing and another, quite different thing is the forms that it acquires in each particular culture or age.

This process accelerated in the nineteenth century, especially toward its end, when it culminated in the appearance and development of avant-garde movements. The poets who took themselves seriously became more and more keen on being faithful to poetry itself, but not necessarily to the contingent or accidental appearances that it has taken in a certain place, at a certain time. They therefore tended to think that, inasmuch as such and such conventions pretended to be essential to poetry, they were in fact concealing or distorting its real essence. Hence it became imperative for them to discard such conventions, doing away with, as Blanchot says, the distinctions and the limits, so as to allow poetry to assert itself in its essence. Thus, the real poet rebelled not only against the conventional forms of poetry but also against the conventional perception of poetry. Such conventional perception and forms had been taken as natural by the false poet and the Philistine. And, conventionally, poetry belonged among the amenities of life. Against such a domesticated conception of poetry, the real poet imposed on himself a double task: on the one hand, to dismantle the conventions that elided or tamed poetry and, on the other hand, to allow poetry to appear in its essential and savage state. I believe that such was, in most cases, the utopian perspective of late nineteenth- and early twentieth-century avant-garde poets.

The avant-garde is almost always associated with rupture, and Paz's phrase "tradition of rupture" is often used to describe it. In the last analysis, this expression implies that the avant-garde practices rupture for its own sake (*la rupture pour la rupture*). No doubt there are movements that correspond to such a description, but it would be too superficial to pretend to use it to describe *the* avant-garde. In the first place, the avant-gardes are very different from each other. In the second place, ruptures are very different from each other. When a certain work of art breaks with some tradition, this does not necessarily mean that the rupture itself must be taken as its most important motive or accomplishment. Mallarmé, for instance, indicates that he wrote "Un coup de dés" in order to explore the relations between constellations of letters, words, phrases, fonts, and the void in the space-time of the page, on which these elements become manifestations of the "prismatic subdivisions of the Idea." If this meant breaking with the verse, such a rupture was a mere side effect of such an experience. In fact, in a preface to "Un coup de dés," he states that the genre of poetry he had just created "leaves intact ancient verse."[13]

Thus, rupture is not always the result of the desire to break with all tradition. It sometimes represents, on the contrary, a wish to re-establish a link with a repressed or neglected tradition. Ezra Pound and T. S. Eliot, for instance, are considered modernist not because of their affinity with modern times but simply because the poetry they produced broke with the way poetry was then being done, which to them seemed worn out and predictable in its forms, themes, images, and dictions. Since, in their eyes, such poetry was the result of the decadence or dilution of tradition, they decided to redeem tradition from such an ignoble seizure. Clearly this could not be achieved through its servile copy, since such was exactly what decadent poetry had done. On the contrary, what they had to imitate was the spirit in which the great poets of the past had faced their poetical task—that is, taking poetry, for instance, as something still to be rediscovered or reinvented; something enigmatically charged with meaning "to the utmost possible degree"; something at once purer, rougher, and subtler than expected; something so "irrepressibly fresh" that it broke up with what had gone on before; something whose novelty did not wear out.[14]

Let us now consider the experience of the avant-garde as a whole. In the first place, avant-garde poets reveal—less with their manifestoes than with their poems—new paths for poetry. The free verse Walt Whitman practiced, for instance, can be considered an *avant la lettre* avant-garde discovery. This is the first aspect—a positive aspect—of their endeavor. However, in the second place, the production of poems employing forms and means that break with traditional notions, forms, and means shows, once and for all, the accidental character of such traditional means, forms, and notions. We know nowadays that a poem does not have, for instance, to tell any story or myth, that its theme does not have to be "lofty," that it does not have to employ a "noble" vocabulary, that it does not have to use traditional forms, that it does not have to obey any particular metrical scheme, that it does not have to be composed of verses, that it does not have to be rhymed, that it does not have to obey any particular rhythmic scheme, that it does not have to be discursive. It was part of the rhetoric not only of the avant-garde but of its enemies to talk of "destruction," "death," and "end." For instance, while the avant-gardists boasted of having destroyed, killed, or ended, for instance, verse, fixed forms, or such and such grammatical conventions, their enemies deplored such destructions, deaths, or endings. The fact is that, regardless of the ambitions or illusions of their protagonists, none of these things really ceased to exist. Every formal possibility ever discovered is still available and can still be creatively employed. The real feat of the avant-garde was not the closing but the opening of doors. Though in showing new possibilities, the avant-garde relativized traditional possibilities; the fact is that to relativize something is not to destroy it.

Third, the new means, forms, and notions employed by the avant-garde are just as accidental to poetry as the traditional ones. The different avant-garde movements have different—and sometimes incompatible—conceptions of poetry. In spite of this, we are nowadays capable of admiring poems produced by members of antagonistic movements. The fact that, for instance, the theses of the surrealist avant-garde were incompatible with those of the futurist avant-garde does not preclude us from equally appreciating poems written by surrealist poets as well as poems written by futurist poets. And likewise we can appreciate poems written in the traditions that each of these movements pretended to supplant and bury.

Finally, in the fourth place, if we consider the effect that—*malgré eux-mêmes*—the avant-garde movements as a whole had, we must say that they have forced us to expand our notion of poetry. We now know that it is not the obedience to this or that particular rule, not the adoption of this or that form, not the pertinence to this or that genre that warrants the artistic quality of a poem. What would we think of a poet or critic who nowadays decreed that only texts composed in metric and rhymed verses are real poems? Or, on the contrary, that only what is written in free verses is a poem? Or that only sequences of sentences are poems? We now know that, in principle, it is not possible to decree what is admissible and what is inadmissible in a poem. Consequently, we know that it is not possible to establish a priori criteria by which all poems must be appraised. The modern poet—and "modern" at this point means *living at a time when the experience of the avant-garde has been accomplished*—is not only capable of employing whatever forms she chooses for her poems but must be aware that they never amount to more than a portion of the possible forms. And the modern critic must acknowledge this fact.

According to the description that I have just made of the experience of the avant-garde qua avant-garde, the nature of its main feat was not artistic or aesthetic but purely cognitive and, more precisely, conceptual. In other words, though one cannot say that, after such an experience, poetry has become better than it was before, one can say that, after it, something new has been learned about poetry. An apprenticeship or a disclosure, that is, a cognitive process, has taken place. We now know something important (although of a negative character) about the nature of poetry, something that had not previously been adequately known.

The difference between the artistic accomplishment and the purely conceptual feat of a poem can be illustrated by Rimbaud's poem "Mouvement."[15] Besides being a beautiful poem, "Mouvement" is generally taken to be the first poem written in free verses in the French language. The fact that it was written in free verses is, of course, an artistic or aesthetic option internal to the poem. A critical appreciation of "Mouvement" may try to explain this option in view of structural considerations and may go as far as making value judgments about it, considering the poem as a whole or its theme or its function in the context of the book that it is part of (i.e., *Illuminations*), and so forth. Independently of this, however, since "Mouvement" is taken to be a poem, the sheer fact that it was written in free verse has a purely conceptual consequence, independently of any other consideration one might make about it as a work of art. By its mere existence, it demonstrated that a poem in French does not have to be written in metrical verses. This demonstration has an immense cognitive and historical value. Therefore, thanks to a purely conceptual feat, "Mouvement" is unquestionably one of Rimbaud's most important poems, even if it remains debatable whether it can, from the aesthetic point of view, be considered one of his best works.

Clearly, the purely conceptual value of a work of art lies in what it teaches, not in itself. If something has nothing but a cognitive value, then it is a mere vehicle for what it teaches. As soon as its message is known, the work itself becomes superfluous. Whoever wants to learn the theory of gravity will do better reading a textbook on classical physics than reading Newton's *Principia*, whose original words have a merely historical value. In the same way, someone who has read about Duchamp's "Fontaine" and seen its photographs can dispense seeing a replica (its "original" no longer exists, and its existence was never important anyway). Such a thing could never be said of works of art of real aesthetic value, such as Miró's triptych "Azul," which must be seen, or Mallarmé's sonnet "Salut," which must be read or heard.

To take a work of art that is important from the conceptual point of view as necessarily important from the artistic or aesthetic point of view was a common mistake perpetrated by avant-garde artists and their admirers. On the other hand, not to see that an aesthetic or artistically insignificant work of art

("Fontaine" is the classical example) can have a great conceptual and historical significance was a common mistake perpetrated by avant-garde detractors.

The fact is not only that the main avant-garde feat is conceptual but that the most important thing it teaches can be stated in a few words. The avant-garde has made known, once and for all, that it is not in principle possible to determine either the necessity or the impossibility for poetry to employ any conceivable form. An infinite number of possible but contingent paths have been opened for it. The artistic genre has been exposed as no more than a contingent collection of forms. Poetic forms cannot be based on hereditary or family prerogatives. Each poem—as each work of art—must be considered and judged as an individual, not as a member of a genre, gender, or species. The path to these discoveries—which are really nothing but the unfolding of a single one—has been run through and cannot be extended. In this sense, there is no longer any place for avant-gardes. Their course has been successfully consummated. I believe that this is the real explanation for the fact that the avant-garde project has been, in Haroldo de Campos's words, "succeeded by a plurality of possible poetics." Such is the world we are living in.

6

"Blanco"

A Version of Mallarmé's Heritage

LUIZ COSTA LIMA

Augusto de Campos and Haroldo de Campos famously referred to Joaquim de Sousândrade, a poet whose rediscovery they championed, as a "clandestine earthquake."[1] Staying with this image, one might understand concrete poetry, which the Campos brothers and Décio Pignatari cultivated, to be an overt earthquake. This is so in part because these three made the Poundian motto "make it new" their own but also because they openly kept themselves, following Sousândrade's own expression, outside the choir of the "happy few." In general, the concrete poets worked tirelessly (and publicly) to end Brazil's cultural isolation. In Spanish America, Octavio Paz was their most important partner. The first edition of *Transblanco* contained, besides the original text of the poem "Blanco" and its transcreation into Portuguese, a small anthology of the Mexican poet, his correspondence with Emir Rodríguez Monegal and with the essayist Celso Lafer, and a few fundamental and introductory essays for the reading of "Blanco."

"Blanco": An Elementary Approach

In developing this chapter, I first thought of analyzing *Transblanco* as a dialogue between the concrete poets and Paz's "Blanco." It quickly became clear that such a task would surpass the limits of the space available to me; soon afterward, I concluded that it would be too much even to speak of the whole of "Blanco." In the end, I forced myself to focus on only part of the poem, my goal being to show what it might offer to our understanding of Michel Foucault's reflection on the specificity of Mallarmé's poetics. Given that, for both the concrete poets and Foucault, Mallarmé's "Un coup de dés" is the hallmark of the latter's production, one might expect me to work here to verify the common descent of Paz and the concrete poets from Mallarmé. My goal, however, is different. I argue that while the Foucauldian lineage fits well in the case of Paz, the concrete poets follow a different course, one that I will outline at the end of the present chapter.

My argument consists of two steps. I first seek to illuminate the part of "Blanco" that speaks to the Foucauldian lineage. I then synthesize Foucault's reflection and the conception of poetry that stems from it. As a kind of coda, I reserve a few words for the alternative poetics articulated by Haroldo de Campos in *Galáxias*, a work that is for Campos what "Blanco" is for Paz. It should be noted that, in establishing this parallel between "Blanco" and *Galáxias*, I restrict my argument to Paz and Campos and do not extend it to concrete poetry in general.

The advent of autonomous art corresponds, in poetry as in painting, to the idea that all themes or accidents can be converted into an art object. It is this that we might refer to as a poem's foundational character of which Baudelaire's sonnet "A une passante" is a model. If, however, much of "Blanco" and *Galáxias* tends to be short and sharp, neither work is referred to, except on rare occasions, as foundational. In the case of "Blanco," Paz centers on the relation between world and language, a relation that is nonetheless posed antithetically to the way it is presented and how it functions for Mallarmé. As Eduardo Milán puts it: "In Mallarmé, language swallows the world; in 'Blanco,' it creates it."[2] The proximity of "Blanco" and *Galáxias* to creation myths lies in the fact that they both establish the profound—one could even say ontological—entwinement between two terms, language and world. We might also add that the proximity of the foundational poem to the creation myth serves to disturb the function of mythical language. In so-called primitive societies, the creation myth explains and legitimates a specific social practice; in modernity, such as with Mallarmé's or Paz's foundational poems, the mythical foundation results in the uncertainty that goes along with a throw of the dice or a descent into nothingness.

With matters of myth and foundational poetry in mind, let us examine a few moments from "Blanco." Its opening scene takes up the whole first page, and—as in the Gospel of St. John—one notices immediately that "in beginning was the Word." Unlike the biblical scenario, however, there is here no Being commanding creation. The word is its own seed, existing before its signification:

inocente promiscua
la palabra
sin nombre sin habla

[stainless promiscuous
the word
speechless nameless][3]

As Milán has argued: "Even knowing that the world is previous to the poem, the text, in creating the world, creates its image, its equal."[4] What this means is that instead of the world being the prior condition for linguistic signification, both things—language and world—stand as one another's image. Milán provides another vital point: "In *Blanco*, Paz ends up accepting the lost original equivalence between Word and thing, between language and world. . . . Language created the world along with the impossibility of . . . directly naming it."[5] Thus, Paz's conception openly opposes the biblical one. In the Bible, there is a superior Being that, on saying "Let there be light," creates from the void the thing "light" and, simultaneously, its name. In "Blanco," which is the result of a "disenchanted" vision, for language to be the seed of the world supposes the a priori negation of a substantialist vision of the world. In the face of that world, and with poetry's inability to name it directly, we see the affirmation of another route—metaphysical, theological (in the pre-Kantian conception), or scientific, in a way of thinking that starts most markedly with Descartes. In a disenchanted world, poetry thus assumes the foundational dignity that the Western world had denied it until the end of the eighteenth century.

On the second and third pages of "Blanco," it is worth remarking that language comes up as a stem—from a seed—that emerges from the bowels of the earth:

Escalera de escapulario,
El lenguaje deshabitado.
[The spine of the mineshaft ladder,
Abandoned language.]

Upon turning the page, the reader finds Paz presenting language as the stage of writing. It is described—in one of the most beautiful and obscure images of the poem—as "Un girasol / Ya luz carbonizada? Sobre um vaso / De sombra . . . Ficticia, / Flor . . . Cáliz de consonantes y vocals / Incendiadas" (a sunflower / light charred / in a vase / of shadow . . . the flower, / not seen nor imagined: . . . a yellow chalice / of consonants and vowels, / burning). Without trying to figure out exactly what the passage means, one might say that the word—now emerging from its state as a seed—exchanges its vegetal life for one rooted in orality. It is not converted into a dead sign but rather is born again as a chalice of burning letters.

Moving further through "Blanco," one feels an impulse to quicken the rhythm of analysis. Following this impulse, I wish to highlight several passages. The first is the encounter between world and verbal matter, which assumes the tone of an erotic union:

> Muchacha
> tú ríes—desnuda
> en los jardines de la llama
> La pasión de la brasa compasiva
> [Girl
> you laugh—naked
> in the gardens of the flame
> The passion of compassionate coals]

Here there is a darkening of that which is yet to be born that corresponds to the darkness of what is declared. The reference to Mexico—"Castillas de arena, naipes rotos / Y el jeroglífico (agua y brasa) / En el pecho de Mexico caído. / Polvo soy de aquellos lodos. / Río de sangre, / Río de historias" (Castiles of sand, / shredded playing cards, / and the hieroglyph (water and ember) dropped on the chest of Mexico. / I am the dust of that silt. / River of blood, river of histories)—associates the foundation of the poem with its place of origin. The dual relation, world and language, becomes ternary: the agent is said through the place from which it speaks and sees. This is so because, contrary to the timeless spatiality of "Un coup de dés," "Blanco" consistently makes evident the place from where one speaks: blood and death are part of its poetic horizon:

> Hablar
> mientras los otros trabajan
> es pulir huesos
> [To speak
> while others work
> is to polish bones]

In this way, the naming of the place (Mexico), not in the biographic sense but as a point of orientation for the development of the poem, fuses into the genetic-erotic aspect of sexual union and of bones. With this, the poem gains a sense of lateral expression—contrary to narrative linearity—while at the same time, through the compression of the expressional planes, its obscurity becomes denser. The *trobar clus* (closed form), which harasses the reader and feeds his or her curiosity, is a forceful consequence of the poem's progress, of its superposition of planes. If the erotic vestige of the world safely contains verses with the quality of "delta de brazos del deseo / en un lecho de vértigos" (delta of arms of desire / on a bed of vertigo), then in the following block of text in "Blanco," land/earth, seen as "lenguaje calcinado" (a language burnt to dust), calls for a plurality of readings. A syntactically contrastive reading—the page that opens with "los ríos de tu cuerpo / país de latidos / entrar en ti / país de ojos cerrados" (the rivers of your body / land of pulse-beats / to enter you / land of closed eyes) leads to "un lecho de vértigos," not to say to the lull of "La transparencia es todo lo que queda" (Transparency is all that remains)—is antithetical to the block of text that follows, which, beginning with "Paramera abrasada" (Desert smoldering), ends with "Este sol es injusto" (This sun is unjust). The contrasts are not posed for the reader to choose from among them but to enhance the effect of dissonance and of the disintegration of reading. Supposing, then, that it would be valid to take blocks of text (or pages) as generators of dissonance, one might turn to the tenth and eleventh pages of the Brazilian edition. These offer the "Inminencia de violencias violetas" (Impending violet violences) as part of the relationship between language and a world of "Tambores tambores tambores" (Drumbeats drumbeats drumbeats) and the agency of language in its battle with the world: "Te golpeo cielo" (Sky I beat you).[6] Directly afterward, one reads about the stresses and tensions between language and the world imbued with the positive characteristic of germinative openness:

tierra revientas
tus semillas estallan
verdea la palabra
[you burst, land,
your seeds explode,
the word grows green]

Without referring to this play of contrasts, a generator of a dissonance that does not diminish, and regarding the passage that begins "Tierra te golpeo" (land I beat you), Julio Ortega argues: "The defiance comes from language and is within language. It is the language of space that permits the conversion of the object (from the word) into a symbol of fecundity and of the subject into the bearer of the verbal seed. The defiance is thus resolved on the page as in the final cosmos of language."[7]

The interpretative outline I present here is of course highly provisional. It seems possible to say that the superposition of discontinuous blocks of text, the contiguity of contrasting plans, and the obscurity ingrained in the resulting poem result not only from the foundational character of "Blanco" but also from the fact that between language and world there is a simultaneous coming-together/interaction and interruption/discontinuity. These two points, at least in "Blanco," are not radically separated from one another. For this reason, one finds the erotic-corporeal conjunction and the separation of what is unrealized occurring side by side:

habitar tu nombre *despoblar tu cuerpo*
caer en el grito contigo *casa del viento*
La irrealidad de lo mirado
da realidad a la mirada
[to inhabit your name *to depopulate your body*
to fall in your shriek with you *house of the wind*
The unreality of the seen
brings reality to seeing]

This is still, then, the intermittent game of Yes and No, and the contact between human agent and the word—"falo el pensar y vulva la palabra" (thought phallus and word womb)—supposes a radiant center of fertility:[8]

En el centro
del mundo del cuerpo del espíritu
la grieta el resplandor
[At the center
of the world of the body of the spirit
the cleft the splendor]

Such magnificence—a kind of pre-Edenic world stripped of a punishing God—does not make explicit the dialectics spurred by the agency of the word, *la palabra*:

Sí
es una palabra
aire son nada
son
este insecto
revoloteando entre las líneas
de la página
inacabada
inacabable
[Yes
is a word
they are air nothing

they are
  this insect
fluttering among the lines
on an unfinished
                unfinishable
                        page]

The word produces the world, and with it its nothingness and the insect that flies over the *unfinishable* page. As Milán has stated, although in other terms: word and world remain in contention because one does not take over the other or take on the other's form.[9] In the beginning there was nothingness, and nothingness, in the end, reconstructs itself. Saying it straightforwardly, the impossibility of matching world and language means that the poetic word does not have a referent that might fix it succinctly to the language of the world. Or it might be that it does have a referent, but it differs from the common usage of the word as there is no stable referent. These two possibilities—not having a referent or having a referent that is in a state of permanent instability—foreshadows Foucault's conception of the poetic as well as the alternative that I now briefly outline.

Les mots et les choses: The Peculiarity of the Poetic Word

Curiously and coincidentally, Foucault published *Les mots et les choses* (*The Order of Things*, 1966) in the same year that Paz wrote "Blanco." This makes it impossible to speculate on the possibility of Foucault directly influencing Paz; however, it is more likely that the two authors shared a common intellectual horizon. Let us consider, for example, the importance of Mallarmé for Foucault's conception of the poetic and the extreme analytical quality of Paz's approach to the "Sonnet en yx," published in 1968.

The exemplary position that *Les mots et les choses* occupies in the contemporary historical-philosophical scene results from Foucault's attempt to develop an "archaeology of human sciences," the book's subtitle. In *Les mots et les choses*, he seeks to verify how the relation between language and reality had existed over historical time, through a *longue durée* followed by two discontinuities. The *longue durée* lasts until the end of the sixteenth century and is marked by the centrality of the figure of similitude. As Foucault declares in the opening of chapter 2, "Until the end of the sixteenth century, similitude played a constructive role in the knowledge of Western culture. . . . And representation—were it feast or knowledge—offered itself as repetition: Theater of life or mirror of the world was the title of all language, its mode of announcing itself and formulating its right to speak."[10] From the seventeenth century onward, "the profound interdependence of language and world is undone. The primacy of writing is suspended. The uniform layer in which the *seen* and the *read*, the visible and the enunciable indefinitely intertwine vanishes. Words and things will be severed. . . . Speech will have then as its goal to say what it is, but it won't be anything of what it says."[11] Once the primacy of similitude is dissolved, one can no longer affirm that "the names (were) posed over what they designated, like power is written on the body of the lion."[12] The great discontinuity thus appears, with the Cartesian critique of similitude marking the kick-off of a new epistème in the middle of the seventeenth century and the end of the *longue durée* of the classical age. The self replaces the old belief in the substantiality that underlies the things of the world, and the latter is dissolved in the reflection exercised by the human agent. The individual subject stands as scientific objectivity's last safeguard.[13] For Foucault, the classical era exposes the first stage of the sign's "new disposition," a stage in which we have remained.[14]

The primacy of representation, one might say, comes to stand in for the stability formerly maintained by the similitude between words and things, a stability guaranteed by the support of the divine gaze. If, with Descartes, the role of the *cogito* and the privilege reserved for geometrical figures still admits the certainty of human knowledge, by the end of the eighteenth century, the representational systems, particularly verbal language, are no longer considered sufficient to speak of reality. A few decades later, at the beginning of the nineteenth century, the installation of modernity initiates what is commonly referred to as "the crisis of representation." This is the second discontinuity that Foucault describes. The awareness of this crisis becomes stronger in the second half of the twentieth century, with the assertion that the components of the sign, the signifier and signified, are inherently inadequate. It is true that Ferdinand de Saussure had already stressed the arbitrary character of the verbal sign, but this was largely forgotten, so to speak. By the second half of the twentieth century, however, theorists and avant-garde artists were actively underscoring the inadequacy and arbitrarity of the verbal sign.

This brief summary helps clarify and verify the role that Foucault reserves for literature, and especially poetry, within the process by which the certainty that language previously provided is lost. In chapter 2 he writes: "In a certain sense, we can say that 'literature,' such as it has constituted itself and was designated in the interior of modern times, manifests the return, where it was not expected, of the living being of language."[15] It is a statement whose meaning becomes clearer if we collate it with Foucault's reading of *Don Quixote*. Quixote's madness goes against the poet's grain: he is the "one that, under the differences daily named and predicted, finds again the kinship underlying things, their scattered similitude."[16] Once the supposed solidarity of the sign's components is undone, the poet—foreshadowed by Miguel de Cervantes's prose—anticipates that which, at the height of modernity (that is, in Mallarmé's poetic work), will be particular to the poet. With the poet, "language" arises "in an act of writing that designates nothing beyond itself."[17] The same statement is reaffirmed on the following pages in Foucault's text: "What is it then, this language that says nothing, that never shuts and is called 'Literature'?"[18] The poet radicalizes the awareness of the arbitrariness of the sign, emphasizes its fragile vibration, and abolishes the signifier's referential counterpart (i.e., meaning). Here, as Foucault argues, one finds a proximity to Friedrich Nietzsche: "With Nietzsche, with Mallarmé, thought has been brought back, and violently, to language itself, to its only and difficult being."[19] The crisis of representation supposes for Foucault both the dissociation between sign and sense and the dissociation between utterance and the agent of utterance. "Who speaks in the word?" Foucault asks, before providing his own answer: "Not the meaning of the word, but its enigmatic and precarious being"—a statement that, uncomfortably, seems to echo the Heidegger of "Die Sprache spricht."[20]

Although Foucault does not declare it, the abyss that opens between sound and sense presupposes the suspension of reference. It occurs in the questioning of the relation between who speaks and what is said. According to Foucault, to the question, "Who speaks?" Mallarmé answers (and he never ceases revising his answer) that the one who speaks is "in its solitude, in its fragile vibration, in its nothingness, the word itself—not the meaning of the word, but its enigmatic and precarious being."[21] It is worth noting that the possessives in French—*sa (solitude), sa (vibration fragile), son (néant)*—do not designate the subject of the sentence (*qui parle?*) but that which, when beginning the sentence, would seem to be its object: *le mot lui-même*, the word itself. The slippage of the grammatical construction pushes offstage the agent of the utterance, the human subject, whose position comes to be occupied by that which ceases to be a human production and becomes the true subject: the naked word. The poet's language is thus conceived as a world closed on itself. As it would be unimaginable for Foucault to suppose that the "poet's word" might recover the substantialist conception of language and once again point to the primacy of similitude, the poet's word is, therefore, an endeavor of nothingness. And, to stress that such a conception is by no means exclusive to the Foucault of *Les mots et les choses*, one might consider Jacques Derrida, even at the very moment when his relationship with Foucault crumbled. In a 1970 essay, "La double séance," Derrida would write: "Literature is at once assured and menaced by standing on its own, in the air, alone, away from being, 'and, if you want, alone, with the exception of everything.'"[22] Personal animosity, it seems, would not prevent their conception of poetry from remaining close.

Why This Approach?

I should like now to synthesize what I have developed in the previous pages into four short propositions. First, long before Foucault, before such a reading of contemporary poetry became widespread, and even before Western thinkers began to speak of a "crisis of representation," the post-Baudelairean poetic tradition (in Europe and the Americas) was well aware of what Walter Benjamin had referred to as "Chockerlebnis," "the experience of shock." This was a response to a progressively dynamic, if not chaotic, world in which human relations become ever more anonymous and compiled in the muddle of urban masses. From a purely verbal standpoint, the experience of shock is characterized by the exploration of the sign lying somewhat outside of its quotidian and usual meaning. It is on the broad horizon of the post-Baudelairean poem that the small space occupied by what I have called the foundational text is remarkable. And "Blanco," "Un coup de dés," and *Galáxias* are all, I would argue, foundational. As I see them, foundational texts perform an analogous role in the poetic fiction of the present that myths did/do in primarily oral societies.

Second, the throwing away of the referential "literary space," and the reduction of language to the singular domain of writing, where meaning is rendered insignificant by the vibration of the signifier, implies a philosophy of the poetic. According to this framework, the "representational crisis" no longer offers a sufficient synthesis for poetic or pictorial creation. The result is an emptiness that permeates words and detaches them from the world. Third, as I have argued regarding "Blanco," the poem may be written in dark ink, but it is darker still because no sense is engendered by the words that constitute it. It thus becomes a *trobar clus* (a closed form) and noncontingent. In other words, decoding it would be nothing more than a ridiculous transgression.

Finally, the rupture of the conventional connection between sound and sense does not necessarily lead poetry to be confused with a fragile vibration; rather, it is *un acte d'écrire qui ne désigne rien de plus que soi*, an act of writing that designates nothing more than the self, an act whose meaning would be, consequently, absolutely open and—in other words—undecidable. Not wishing that the contradiction I pose here be taken as a praise of clarity at all cost, I should like to conclude by saying that from the same Baudelairean and Mallarméan heritage derives another and very distinct conception of poetic fiction. For reasons of economy, I restrict myself to referring to the well-known theorization of the fictional by Wolfgang Iser.

According to Iser, literary fiction, even as it goes counter to that which, in psychological tests, is called "good continuation," supposes a formulation of text and space on the page. Its structure is thus composed of full lines—the textual formulation of the work—that are constantly interrupted by empty spaces (*Leerstellen*). While a solver of puzzles would fill the empty spaces with the words expected by the game's creator, in the realm of the poetic it falls to the reader to fill in the *Leerstellen*. That is, the reader introduces connections between discontinuous verbal segments (if one likes, to read between the lines and between words) to form meaning. Such meaning, no doubt, is always plural, since the filling out is always unpredictable: there are wrong connections, for sure, but there is also not a singularly right one.[23] Following Iser, it is fair to conclude that I alone am responsible for the introduction of elements that push this chapter away from Foucault's terrain and into reader reception. But as a last word, I should add that my reading assumes a marked difference between Paz's and Campos's foundational texts: while "Blanco" consistently adjusts itself to French theory, in *Galáxias* there is a textual openness that immediately negates any such adjustment.

7

Translation and Radical Poetics

The Case of Octavio Paz and the Noigandres

ODILE CISNEROS

In the history of literary contacts between Latin America and Brazil, the case involving Haroldo de Campos and Octavio Paz is perhaps one of the most interesting examples of theoretical exchange on translation and avant-garde poetics.[1] Their dialogue exhibits remarkable similarities in their theoretical approach to translation and also considerable differences in their practice, especially, in the translation of radical poetics. In this chapter I explore those parallels, beginning with the dialogue that led to Haroldo de Campos's Portuguese translation of Paz's book-poem "Blanco." On the other hand, I show how, despite the conceptual affinities, practice—particularly in the case of Paz—strays substantially from theoretical pronouncements. I illustrate this hypothesis by analyzing Campos's translation of "Blanco" and translations of Mallarmé and ee cummings authored by Paz and by Haroldo's brother, Augusto de Campos. I thus expand my analysis to encompass the translation practice of the Noigandres group, composed of the Campos brothers and Décio Pignatari, who frequently collaborated on translation projects. This fascinating journey through what I call the Lost & Found Department of literary translation can be seen not only as an important instance of intercultural dialogue but also, with regard to Paz, as a cautionary tale of missed opportunities.[2]

The intellectual dialogue between the two poets officially began in February 1968, when Campos wrote to Paz regarding a series of translations of Paz's poems he was working on for an article by Celso Lafer, a political scientist and writer who had been a student of Paz's at Cornell in 1966.[3] Campos's queries on certain terms led to a lively exchange that culminated in Campos's translation of Paz's "Blanco" more than a decade later.[4] In his initial letter, Campos remarked that in his reading of *Libertad bajo palabra*, he had noticed a poetics that substantially differed from the "metaphorical and rhetorical-discursive tradition" characterizing Spanish and Spanish American poetry in this century.[5] Campos was referring to what he termed "the brief, stripped-down poems, related to haiku and to montage syntax; and also poems dealing with the mechanics of the poem—metalinguistic poems, . . . in which poetry is made from its own makings."[6] For the Brazilian, those poems stood closer to Mallarmé's "Coup de dés" and to Paz's radical theoretical exposé outlined in the epilogue to the French edition of *El arco y la lira* (*The Bow and the Lyre*). Along with his letter, Campos also sent Paz a copy of *antologia noigandres* and *Teoria da poesia concreta*, the first samplings of the radical poetry and theoretical writings the Noigandres group was beginning to produce in the mid-1950s.

In his reply, Paz acknowledged having heard of Brazilian concrete poetry through his dialogue with ee cummings, whose poems were being translated by Augusto, Haroldo's brother.[7] But Paz (who had also tried his hand at translating cummings, as I will discuss more below) only seriously began to consider the principles of concrete poetry after his contact with Campos. Despite his openness to the new poetics coming out of Brazil, Paz took issue with Campos's characterization of Spanish and Spanish American poetry as a "rhetorical-discursive tradition."[8] Paz did not see Campos's remark as inaccurate—he objected, however, to its "dismissive tone" and politely pointed out that this was the tradition of a "great living poetry," one that was not exclusive to the Spanish language. Pound, Eliot, Stevens, Apollinaire, St. John Perse, Pessoa, and Mayakovski, among others, Paz observed, had also cultivated the long poem. Still, Paz praised the unique linguistic space the concrete poets were staking out and confessed that "very few works of poetry in recent years have afforded me the joy and surprises I found in your poems, Augusto de Campos's, Décio Pigantari's and your other friends."[9] Paz's admiration was later translated into *Topoemas*, a poetic homage he dedicated to the Brazilian concrete poets, incorporating their lessons. With his letter, Paz enclosed a copy of his own long poem "Blanco," where he acknowledged the use of the same type of montage syntax practiced by the concrete poets.

Interestingly enough, at that point in time, Campos was already moving away from purely visual concrete poetry. In the style of *Finnegans Wake*,

Campos's new work, *Galáxias*, was a poetic prose, or "proesia," that laid a particular emphasis on sound. After Joyce, he entitled the first few fragments "prosa en progresso" (prose in progress). In his next letter to Paz, Campos explained that beyond the elimination of syntax through montage techniques advocated by their manifesto "pilot plan for concrete poetry" (published in 1958), the Noigandres group viewed concrete poetry not simply as a visual experiment but as a semantic and semiotic one as well: "It is a very broad, general approach, a methodical attitude that can go from a single-word poem or one involving artificial visual signs (Décio Pignatari's 'code poetry') to very complex compositions (such as Augusto's color-coded poems or Pignatari's 'Estela cubana' or my own prose in progress)."[10] Campos also mentioned to Paz his book *Metalinguagem*, which contained his seminal essay, "Da tradução como criação e crítica" ("Translation as Creation and Criticism"), although it is unclear whether Paz had access to it at that point.

As I have noted elsewhere, Campos's reflections on translation in "Translation as Creation and Criticism," begun at least six years before his correspondence with Paz, were directly linked to the theory of concrete poetry.[11] Concrete poetry's radical attempts to diminish the gap between signifier and signified and to create close connections between the material and meaning of the poem present a number of challenges for the translator. Consequently, the translation concepts formulated by the Noigandres poets proposed solutions that addressed precisely those challenges. In other words, these concepts considered the translation of such texts as paradigmatic. And just as concrete poetry theory establishes an isomorphic relationship (of formal resemblance) between the form and the meaning of the poem, so do the translation theories postulate a similar isomorphic relationship in which original and translation mirror each other. This is to say that since texts with a highly dense literary texture are "impossible" to translate, the only possible translation in these cases is a translation of their form. In "Translation as Creation and Criticism," Campos stresses the autonomy of translation, highlighting at the same time the isomorphic relationship between translation and original: "Once we admit, in principle, the thesis of the impossibility of translating 'creative' texts, it seems that we may also admit, in principle, the corollary of this thesis, the possibility of recreating the texts. The texts may exist, then, as Bense wishes, in two languages and as two bodies of autonomous aesthetic information, which, we should like to add, will be linked to each other through an isomorphic relation: they will be different in language, but like isomorphic bodies, they will crystallize within the same system."[12]

In 1970, a couple of years after his correspondence with Campos, Paz argued something similar in his essay "The Literal and the Literary."[13] Like Campos, Paz insisted first on the fixed nature of the poem's language when he stated that "the meanings of the poem are multiple and variable; the words of the same poem are unique and cannot be replaced by others. To change them would be to destroy the poem."[14] Despite this view of the fixity of signs in the poem, Paz also admits that translation, while difficult, is not impossible. For Paz, the "task of the translator" would be, "in another language and with different signs . . . to compose a poem that is analogous with the original."[15]

Whether resorting to analogy or isomorphism, both Paz and Campos advocated for literary translation (particularly of poetry in its most radical forms), notwithstanding the apparent (or avowed) fixity of the poem's language, in Paz's case, or in Campos's, the "absolute phrase" of the poem, "which has no content other than its own structure."[16] Both also bring out the critical character of translation. Campos emphatically asserts that "all translation is criticism," and Paz, for his part, writes, "Every reading is a translation and every piece of criticism is, or begins by being, an interpretation."[17] The similarity is striking, especially if we consider that, although Paz's essay came out somewhat later, it is unlikely that he had read Campos's "Da tradução como criação e crítica."

Some years later, in 1978, Campos communicated to Paz his intention of translating Paz's radical simultaneist poem "Blanco," a feat he accomplished three years later and in the course of a single night, as Campos later wrote in an homage poem entitled "Translatio," which he sent to Paz in a letter.[18] Harking back to the chemical concept of isomorphic bodies, Campos called his translation a "diamantização" (diamondization).[19] Paz judged Campos's version to be "better and more concis[e] than the Spanish one," and Julio Ortega has noted how Campos's text demonstrates that "translation is not only creative and critical, but it also implies a combinatory activity that unleashes mechanisms that are unexpected or maybe are latent in language."[20]

Two brief examples may perhaps illustrate how Campos captures and radicalizes the possibilities latent in Paz's poem. In a text such as "Blanco," which foregrounds the metaphoric birth of poetry, the line "ánima entre las sensaciones" becomes, in Campos's Portuguese version, "alma animando sensações," which resonates, by Paz's own admission, with precisely the kind of animism he wished to evoke. Likewise, in the telluric motif, "tierra, revientas / tus semillas estallan," Campos substitutes the parallelisms "ie" / "ie" and "illas" / "allan" by "Tremor, / terra desventras, / explodem tuas sementes," creating the alliterations and vowel echoes "tre" / "ter" / "tras" and "o-e" (expl*o*d*e*m) / "e-e" (sem*e*nt*e*s). Semantically, Campos's solution reinforces the allusion to a violent genesis underlying Paz's images: for instance, "revientas" (to explode) becomes "desventras," literally, "to tear apart the belly." From the phonetic and sound angle, Campos's solid formulation seems more attuned to the geological birth of the word, with all its chthonic force. Perhaps because of the subtle way Campos links sound to sense, he at times achieves in Portuguese what Paz's Spanish can only hint at. In other words, Campos's detailed attention to the connections between sound and meaning are crucial to achieve the same effect, or a better one, in Portuguese. A thankful Paz also acknowledged Campos's achievements in the department of rhythm and other sound devices: "As for the rhythm, which is the most difficult thing to translate, the greatest obstacle that we all face as translators of poetry: as far as I can judge, I think you managed to completely replicate the polymetric character of the original. Another notable feat is that you found equivalencies for the alliteration, paronomasia, and other verbal echoes."[21]

The affinity between Paz and Campos also extended to the material they translated. Steeped in the radical poetics of the twentieth century, it is no surprise that both Paz and the Noigandres poets chose to translate Stephane Mallarmé, universally acknowledged as a forerunner of modern poetry. In the collectively authored volume *Mallarmé* (published in 1974), the Noigandres poets published individual and triple translations (baptized as "triducção," by Décio Pignatari). Both Paz and Augusto de Campos tackled his celebrated "Sonnet en yx," with Paz devoting a brilliant commentary to its complex poetics. While their object choice was similar, the results could not have been more different. I quote below Mallarmé's original, alongside Paz's and Augusto's translations:

Mallarmé:
Ses purs ongles très haut dédiant leur onyx,
L'Angoisse, ce minuit, soutient, lampadophore,
Maint rêve vespéral brûlé par le Phénix
Que ne recueille pas de cinéraire amphore

Sur les crédences, au salon vide: nul ptyx,
Aboli bibelot d'inanité sonore,
(Car le Maître est allé puiser des pleurs au Styx
Avec ce seul objet dont le Néant s'honore).

Mais proche la croisée au nord vacante, un or
Agonise selon peut-être le décor
Des licornes ruant du feu contre une nixe,

Elle, défunte nue en le miroir, encor
Que, dans l'oubli fermé par le cadre, se fixe
De scintillations sitôt le septuor.[22]

Octavio Paz:
El de sus puras uñas ónix, alto en ofrenda,
La Angustia, es medianoche, levanta, lampadóforo,

Mucho vesperal sueño quemado por el Fénix
Que ninguna recoge ánfora cinerario:

Sala sin nadie en las credencias conca alguna,
Espiral espirada de inanidad sonora,
(El Maestro se ha ido, llanto en la Estigia capta
Con ese solo objeto nobleza de la Nada).

Mas cerca la ventana vacante al norte, un oro
Agoniza según talvez rijosa fábula
De ninfa alanceada por llamas de unicornios

Y ella apenas difunta desnuda en el espejo
Que ya en las nulidades que claüsura el marco
Del centellar se fija súbito el septimio.[23]

Augusto de Campos:
Puras unhas no alto ar dedicando seus ônix,
A Angustia, sol nadir, sustem, lampadifária,
Tais sonhos vesperais queimados pela Fênix
Que não recolhe, ao fim, de ânfora cinerária

Sobre áreas, no salão vazio: nenhum ptyx,
Falido bibelô de inanição sonora
(Que o Mestre foi haurir outros prantos no Styx
Com esses único ser de que o Nada se honora).

Mas junto à gelosia, ao norte vaga, um ouro
Agoniza talvez segundo o adorno, faísca
De licornes, coices de fogo ante o tesouro,

Ela, defunta nua num espelho embora,
Que no olvido cabal do retângulo fixa
De outras cintilações o séptuor sem demora.[24]

While a thorough analysis of these translations would be outside the scope of this chapter, note, for example, how Paz almost completely abandons the sonic possibilities of rhyme, which is precisely the poem's tour de force and what inspired its unofficial title. On the other hand, Augusto, while recognizing the impossibility of finding six rhymes in "yx," aims to approximate the sounds through inversions and parallelisms, as in "faísca" and "fixa," and "Falido bibelô." Incorporating the rhymes does not mean slavishly giving in to a mere historical poetic convention. As Augusto points out in his essay "Mallarmé: O poeta em greve" (Mallarmé: The poet on strike): "I paid special attention, in the translation, to word play in Mallarmé's poetry—the paronomasias, assonances, and alliterations—in which rhyme stands out. Mallarmé's rhymes—punning rhymes, homophone rhymes, leonine rhymes, rhymes that echo, devour and mirror each other—contribute decisively to breaking, through their vertical associations, the horizontal chain of the line of verse. I did not hesitate to adopt extreme solutions, which, though sometimes lacking in a particular place of the original, seem to me to be fully justified in Mallarmé's poetics."[25] Augusto's version builds on and extends the possibilities suggested by the original. In contrast, Paz's translation loses in the sound department but still makes some gains in the area of sentence structure. Mallarmé's syntax is complex and deliberately obscure, something that Paz radicalizes. The syntactic inversions of lines such as "el de sus puras uñas ónix" and "mucho vesperal sueño" produce a Mallarmé who is structurally closer to baroque poets such as Góngora, Quevedo, and Sor Juana than to the nineteenth-century Spanish American *modernistas* influenced by Mallarmé and French symbolism. For his part, Augusto tries to compensate for the Parnassian and symbolist rhetorical "excesses" in the Brazilian tradition by giving us, instead, a Mallarmé with a lighter diction, yet not turning him into one of our contemporaries.[26]

The ee cummings poems are another case in point where theory coincides but translations part ways. Both Augusto and Paz began to independently translate cummings in the mid-1950s (Augusto in 1954 and Paz in 1955). In their respective essays, "Intradução de cummings" (a pun on "introdução" [introduction] and "tradução" [translation]) and "Siete poemas y un recuerdo de ee cummings" (Seven poems and a memory of ee cummings), both noticed cummings's radical approach to poetry, his individualism, and his rebelliousness, all coupled with formal perfection. Referring specifically to "l(a," a poem they both translated, Augusto remarks on the text's precision, calling it cummings's "most perfect poem . . . one of the densest images of solitude, in what could be called 'a haiku of the falling leaf.'"[27] Similarly, Paz observes that cummings's poems are "the children of calculation at the service of passion" (hijos del cálculo al servicio de la pasión), and that early on he achieved a "perfection that would have to be called incandescent except for the fact that it is freshness personified. Spring in flames" (perfección que no habría más remedio que llamar incandescente si no fuese al mismo tiempo la frescura en persona. Primavera en llamas).[28] The surprising resemblance of these interpretations (most probably made independently) is, however, not echoed in the translation of this singular poem or in the choice of other poems they translated.

While Augusto recognizes the delicate—or "calculated, " to use Paz's term—architecture of the poem and tries to re-create it not only at the semantic and phonetic levels but also with regard to typography, Paz instead chooses a transposition that respects the graphic layout but does not radicalize or update its rich potential. A comparison of the versions is instructive:

ee cummings:

l(a

le
af
fa

ll

s)
one
l

iness

Augusto de Campos:

so	**l**(a
(l	le
f	af
o	fa
l)**l**	ll
(ha	s)
c	**one**
ai)	**l**
itude	**iness**

Octavio Paz:

s(u

na
ho
ja

ca
e)
o
l

edad[29]

A horizontal transposition of cummings's poem reveals the phrase "(a leaf falls)" inside the word "loneliness." Paz's calque reproduces this structure perfectly. By linguistic coincidence, perhaps, it is admirable that the length of words in Spanish, as well as the position where the vowels occur, allows Paz to generate other parallels: two-letter lines in the first three stanzas and the coincidence of the letter *l* in the fifth line. The first three stanzas create an equilibrium with the same number of vowels and consonants while also respecting the semantics. In sum, Paz achieves a translation that is elegant and, in a sense, classical.[30]

Augusto, on the other hand, does not hesitate to unleash and even radicalize the potentialities of cummings's poem. As he states in a detailed analysis that I can only summarize here, the phrase and word composing the poem oppose a subjective concept (loneliness) to an objective image (a leaf falls).[31] The original contains twenty letters in total: four vowels occurring eight times, and four consonants occurring twelve times. Both the word and the sentence have the same number of letters (i.e., ten). The composition is organized into stanzas or "line groups" that alternate between one and three lines. In the second stanza, alternating consonants and vowels suggest, iconically, the zigzag motion of the falling leaf, making a brief pause in the middle stanza, "ll." The sign "l" is deliberately ambiguous, as it may correspond to both the letter *l* and the number 1. This is further highlighted by the division of the word into "l-one-l-iness," as the number appearing twice is isolated, and this also generates the words "one" and "iness," something like "I-ness," an allusion to the identity, unity, or uniqueness of the ego. This also brings out isolation (loneliness) as one of the themes of the poem.

Augusto's solution is based on the above close, almost microscopic reading. His translation, as he himself admits, has fewer letters (sixteen) and two parentheses more; five vowels occurring eight times and seven consonants that also occur eight times. With a sense of mathematical equivalence, Augusto tries to compensate for the use of more consonants and vowels (instead of four and four) with the same number of occurrences (eight and eight). Spatialization also produces readings on several levels: in particular, the word "so" can be read as "só" (only, lonely, one, etc.), and "ai)" is the Portuguese phonetization of the English word "I." Going further, the curly font and the colors Augusto chose (by the Dutch typography firm Mecanorma) allowed him to, "through association, . . . contaminate with some leaves other letters (the isolated Cs and Os), as well as the privileged Ls and Fs, [giving] the illusion of recuperating some of the lost iconicity" of cummings's poem.[32] Finally, what he calls an "an eye for errata" allows the reader to discover the word "haicai" (haiku) in the fourth stanza, thus inscribing the poem within that venerable Japanese poetic tradition. In sum, Augusto's translation goes to great lengths to exploit the possibilities of the original exponentially.

A contrast too is apparent in the poems Paz and Augusto chose to translate. Besides the emphasis on word fragmentation illustrated above, Augusto privileged poems playing on sound. Consider, for example, how Augusto's translation of "my specialty is living said" explores the sonic possibilities suggested by the original:

my specialty is living said
a man (who could not earn his bread
because he would not sell his head)

squads right impatiently replied
two billion pubic lice inside
one pair of trousers (which had died)

minha especialidade é viver—era a legenda
de um homem (que não tinha renda
porque não estava à venda)

olhar à direita—replicaram num segundo
dois bilhões de piolhos púbicos do fundo
de um par de calças (moribundo)

Here Augusto correctly perceives how the original contrasts the short vowel rhyme of first triplet / ed / with the long vowel one / aid / of the second triplet and transforms this into parallel rhymes in -enda and -undo. Augusto does this without compromising the meaning, and even enhances it. For example, he renders the ordinary word "said" as "legenda," meaning label, photo caption, movie subtitles, or inscription in Portuguese. Besides incorporating that word's rich polysemy, the translation humorously highlights the sententious nature of the protagonist's words "my specialty is living," elevating them from a simple utterance to a life dictum. The word "moribundo" (moribund or dying) has the effect of personifying the pair of trousers, accentuating the humor of the rather simple "which had died." In contrast to these elaborations, a certain shyness or solemnity comes through in Paz's nonrhymed version of cummings's delightful "love is thicker than forget," making the end result not only less appealing to the ear but also semantically less playful.[33]

By way of conclusion, I suggest that what Paz himself said regarding the stance of the poet as translator often applies to Paz's translations. Paz argues that "poets rarely make good translators. The reason is that they almost always use the foreign poem as a point of departure for writing one of their own."[34] This is an attitude Paz himself often exemplifies. His cummings translations abandon many of the original playful and childlike features and lose on sound quality. They also appear stripped of the frank eroticism characterizing some of cummings's poems, a curious omission given Paz's great interest in the subject.[35] The complex rhymes of Mallarmé's "Sonnet en yx" are sacrificed and substituted by syntactic inversions and what appears an inadequate compensation through the use of blank verse. Still, Paz's version should be credited with some notable finds, as is the translation of the famous line "abolition bibelot d'inanité sonore" as the imaginative "espiral espirada de inanidad Sonora," or the use of the word "conca" for the mysterious term "ptyx." But we should perhaps not judge Paz too harshly, a license he himself calls for in the preface to the volume of his translations, eloquently titled *Versiones y diversiones* (roughly,

Versions and diversions). As that volume reveals, Paz also viewed his translation praxis as an entertaining "diversion," a fun exercise as much a distraction or diversion from his "serious" work in poetry or essays. His "versions," unlike those of Haroldo and Augusto, do not claim the same status as their originals or independence from them. Tellingly, Paz did not include *Versiones y diversiones* as a volume of his *Complete Works*.

The Noigandres group, unlike Paz, not only theoretically but also practically attempted to elevate translation to the level of creation and demystify the fetish of originality. The Campos brothers published many translations as part of their work. Augusto de Campos's book of translations, *Poesia da Recusa* (Poetry of denial) (2006), which explores the idea of both aesthetic and ethical denial in poetry, also implies a denial of "originality," since, the author argues, the translator should "identify with the text and abdicate an[y] entirely premeditated plan."[36] In "Da razão antropofágica" ("Anthropophagous Reason: Dialogue and Difference in Brazilian Culture"), an essay written in 1981, the same year as *Transblanco*, Haroldo went so far as to question the primacy of ontological origin, and consequently of the original, based on Jacques Derrida's critique of logocentrism and concept of "differánce." Campos's critical position here constitutes an attempt to liberate Latin American culture ("the new barbarians") from the yoke of its European colonial heritage: "Europeans must learn to live together with the new barbarians who, for some time, in an alternative and different context, have been devouring them and making them flesh of their flesh and bone of their bone. They have long been resynthesizing them chemically, though an impulsive and uncontrollable metabolism of difference."[37] Not only is the origin in question; through translation, the original too is subject to a cannibalizing operation that simultaneously pays homage to its "originality" and captures its energy in a kind of cultural recycling. Thus, instead of the proverbial loss plaguing the translator, translation theory and practice provides the Noigandres poets with a store of creative possibilities and mutually enriching cultural exchange, an opportunity that Paz, on the contrary, does not always seize.

Part II

Remembrances

8

Pages, Pageants, Portraits, Prospects

An Austin-atious Remembrance of Haroldo de Campos

CHARLES A. PERRONE

It is a distinct pleasure to be in this space named after the prominent poet-scholar-professor who was so important in my own formation, as he was for so many others in the arts and higher education in the area of literature.[1] In the spring semester of 1981, Haroldo de Campos was Tinker Professor at the University of Texas, Austin. He nicknamed the city "Austineia Desvairada" and used this same moniker as a rubric for a section of his poetry collection *A educação dos cinco sentidos* (1985, *The Education of the Five Senses*).[2] Between 1971—when Haroldo first served as visiting professor in the Department of Spanish and Portuguese—and 1981, Austin grew considerably and became a national, and by some measures international, center for music, fine arts, literature, and alternative culture, sometimes a bit daring or weird. "Austinatious," we might say, to approximate the Portuguese *desvairada*. At the somewhat more placid university, Haroldo taught two classes in 1981: a senior elective, *Prosa brasileira: Correlações transtemporais* (Brazilian Prose: Transtemporal Co-relations), and a graduate seminar, *Semiologia da evolução literária: O modelo barroco e sua produtividade na poesia brasileira* (Semiology of Literary Evolution: The Baroque Model and Its Productivity in Brazilian Poetry).

During his fruitful stay, Haroldo dealt with diverse students, professors in different departments, inter/national poets, and local publishers. The vibrant university and artistic communities impressed the special guest and inspired both academic and creative works on his part. I was a firsthand witness to Haroldo's adventures, not just in the two classes but at book launches, conferences, readings, and other varied encounters as well. Hoping to contribute to the deservedly constant homage to the master Haroldo, it is gratifying to share something of those experiences by way of this personal remembrance.

Even before 1971 Haroldo had been in Austin. His brother Augusto and he did a sort of concrete poetry tour in 1968, beginning at the University of Texas, continuing on to the University of Indiana, home campus of the poet and organizer Mary Ellen Solt, moving on to the University of Wisconsin, where the incomparable Jorge de Sena was teaching, and ending up at New York University. From January to May 1971, Haroldo worked in Austin. One of his advanced students was Albert Bork, who speaks of that semester to this day, and he posted a brief biography to a website for professionals in translation and simultaneous interpretation.[3] In this narrative, Albert reveals that Haroldo suggested a translation as a term paper for his course in "inventive prose." Albert and another quite capable student translated *Memórias sentimentais de João Miramar* by Oswald de Andrade as "Sentimental Memoirs of John Seaborne." The project became a sort of workshop. On Mondays they would meet at Haroldo's apartment to read the versions to him and to Professor Norman Potter, a regular faculty member who had come from São Paulo. In the words of Bork, now a translator in the field of law, it was "a priceless learning experience." The second colleague turned the task into a master's thesis. The *Texas Quarterly*, quite a reputable journal in its day, published the polished translation.[4] Haroldo also asked Albert to translate an essay that would appear as "Hölderlin's Red Word" in the journal *20th Century Studies*.[5] It was reprinted in *Novas*, the grand anthology of Haroldo in English, to which I will return shortly. Recognizing Albert Bork's talent, the Campos brothers proposed that he translate *Serafim Ponte Grande*, an endeavor undertaken together with the then assistant professor K. David Jackson. The book was published as *Seraphim Grosse Pointe*, with a substantial critical segment by Haroldo.[6]

One thing that Albert does not recount in his web posting is that he possesses a reel-to-reel tape recording of Haroldo reading *Galáxias* in its embryonic phase. The Texan never cleaned up the tape nor did he convert it to cassette or any other medium. I include all this about Albert Bork not only to recognize what he achieved but also because it was he who "oriented" me when I arrived at the reception for the Portuguese section in Austin in the fall of 1980. I knew the city well enough, as my father was born there and I have a hundred or so cousins in the area. But the university was something altogether different.

In January 1981 it was my turn to meet Haroldo. The first question he asked me was if I was related to Leyla Perrone-Moisés (a professor of French literature and cultural critic in São Paulo), a natural question in our academic domain. While there may in fact be a distant medieval-clan connection, my reply to Haroldo was a simple no, and we began to talk about his classes, which would provide so much to me and to the group as a whole. The first was the aforementioned *Prosa brasileira: Correlações transtemporais*, the syllabus of which I retained. The course was organized in four blocks, given here in reverse order: (4) From *Epos* to Epiphanies: *O Ateneu* (The Atheneum), *Perto do coração selvagem* (*Near to the Wild Heart*), Oswald de Andrade, Antônio Vieira, et al.; (3) *A magreza estética* (Slender aesthetics): Machado de Assis, Graciliano Ramos, Dionélio Machado; (2) The Hustler-Anthropophagous Novel: *Memórias de um Sargento de Milícias* (*Memoirs of a Militia Sergeant*), *Macunaíma*, *Miramar-Serafim*; and (1) Recovery of *Epos* via Fable, *Iracema*, *Macunaíma*, and "Meu tio o iauaretê" (My Uncle the Jaguar). For discussion of this last item, we were privileged to receive copies of the professor's fundamental article "A linguagem do Iauaretê."[7] Therein, Haroldo interprets the "Tupy-inization" of Portuguese by João Guimarães Rosa and recommends a complete lexical survey of the corresponding words in the story. Some years later I decided to accept the challenge, only to discover that Professor Suzi Sperber of the UNICAMP had already done so, though she chose not to publish it for some reason. So, I went ahead and finished the research—beginning at the renowned Latin American collection of the University of Texas, Austin—to elaborate a new interpretation.[8]

Given the year of publication (2008), this interpretive lexicon was also a homage, a tribute. If this aspect of the 1981 class led to a useful editorial result, I can affirm with confidence that virtually all the other aspects of that class live to this day in our lessons about Brazilian prose fiction. So much of the material found a place in essays published in Luso-Brazilian periodicals and/or in Haroldo's books. We students also received photocopies of the original typescript of Haroldo's study, which has had more impact worldwide than any other of his, in the original and in translation: "Da razão antropofágica" ("Anthropophagous Reason"). The article first appeared in *Colóquio Letras* (1981) in Lisbon, and Maria Tai Wolff, who studied with Haroldo at Yale, did the first English translation.

One can verify as well the continued presence of much of the content of the second University of Texas class led by Haroldo in 1981, the *Semiologia da evolução literária: O modelo barroco e sua produtividade na poesia brasileira*. There was a fair amount of theory and Gregório de Matos in the syllabus. I remember an anecdote: in the first module of the document I made an addition by hand. It went: "Spivak, introduction to the English translation of *De la grammatologie* by Derrida." This was an essential item that Haroldo must have decided to add after arriving in Austin and realizing that the celebrated Gayatri Spivak was professor of comparative literature there. After he made this assignment, I went to a social gathering for graduate students. A woman standing next to me inquired something about the keg of beer and asked me who I was. I responded and returned the question. The reply? Gayatri Spivak! What convergence, and what prescience Haroldo had had. Soon after we would hear his magisterial application of deconstruction in his defense of the Brazilian baroque in poetry, which also became a book.[9] When I later saw a photograph of Haroldo with Derrida at the home of Leyla Perrone in São Paulo I thought: Gayatri Spivak should be there to savor some Brazilian beer.[10]

For my part, I was quite pleased when Haroldo presented in class the song "Outras Palavras" (Other words) by Caetano Veloso, which contains the line "Quase João Gil muito Ben mas barroco como eu" (Almost João Gil very Ben but baroque like me). There was my term paper topic. The essay, to my delight, was approved by the professor and destined for both North American and Brazilian publications.[11] It is difficult to convey how much this support and encouragement have meant to me.

But enough about classes and papers. What to say about all the other hours of the "austinatious" days about town? I believe that Haroldo's greatest joy was having done and presented the "transcreation" of "Blanco" by the poet-thinker Octavio Paz, a story told in the book *Transblanco* (1986). The *carnaval* of 1981 for Haroldo was rendering Paz's profound long poem, a quasi-mystical February experience leading to a circumstantial poem, titled "Translatio," in a letter to Paz:

> a chamada nébula Caranguejo
> uma constelação de reversos
> na desgaláxia dos buracos negros
> ou a órbita excêntrica de Plutão
> meditada em Austin Texas
> num party em Lavaca Street
> tomei a mescalina de mim mesmo
> e passei esta noite em claro
> traduzindo "Blanco" de Octavio Paz[12]
> [the so-called crab nebulae
> a constellation of reversals
> in the disgalaxy of black holes
> or the excentric orbit of Pluto
> meditated in Austin Texas

at a party on Lavaca Street
I took the mescaline of myself
and I stayed up til dawn
translating "Blanco" by Octavio Paz].

Tellingly, I do not recall if I was actually at said party, but I do know that the definitive version of the poem was published in 1985 with the title "Transblanco" and with only uppercase letters being in the cited title of the translated poem. In the index of *A educação dos cinco sentidos*, the sequence "Austineia Desvairada" has fifteen items, which corresponds to the number of weeks in a semester in the United States. Could this have been intentional? A poem a week in the austinatious host city? Something similar to *Pauliceia Desvairada* (1921), which has twenty-one poems, and twenty-two with the addition of the "Enfibraturas" at the end for the 1922 Week of Modern Art? Pure coincidence? Perhaps.

On March 27, 1981, in a session of the twentieth meeting of the Instituto Internacional de Literatura Iberoamericana in Austin, Haroldo spoke about the transcreation of Paz and read select parts. During the discussion, I asked how he had dealt with the translation of the title Spanish word *blanco*, which has the equivalent *branco* (white) in Portuguese—a convenient allusion to the *espaço-em-branco* (white space) of Brazilian concrete poetry—but where the Spanish term also means *alvo* (target), where the Castillian *albo* is a poetic synonym of *blanco*. At one point, it was reported that the Brazilian book would contain the transcription of the question-and-answer period, but it seems there was excessive material.

Among other things that I found in old boxes while preparing for this presentation were some severely faded sheets of paper containing the translation I did of a talk Haroldo gave. The identification was simply "UT event," but it could have been either the Iberoamerican conference or a special workshop on translation a month later. That symposium was co-organized by Haroldo and explicitly on the occasion of the visit he was making as Tinker Professor. At this event, as K. David Jackson explains elsewhere, "The act of writing was meant to accelerate to galactic speeds." This is a clear allusion to the complete project of the *Galáxias*, which was still unpublished in book form. In early 1981 the only part in published English translation was "passtimes & killtimes" in *Via* by Christopher Middleton and Norman Potter.[13] In Austin, the poet-professor from Peru Julio Ortega collaborated with Haroldo, especially on *Transblanco*. In an anthology of international letters co-edited with Ewing Campbell, *The Plaza of Encounters*, they published another translated "galactic" segment, "here i begin" by Suzanne Jill Levine.[14] Having studied with Emir Rodríguez Monegal and met Haroldo in 1978 when he was visiting professor at Yale, she received a working version of a rendering of the first galaxy to polish into a definitive version. Julio Ortega later published the translation of an interview he did with Haroldo in Austin.[15] Therein the very theme of transcreation is highlighted and the stars of Austin still shine. It must have been in an austinatious moment that Haroldo suggested that I also translate a galactic segment, which did occur, though it remained for years in a drawer. My version of segment 32 "na coroa de arestas" ("on the jagged crown") finally appeared in *Novas Selected Writings*.[16] The co-editor Odile Cisneros, an extreme fan of *Galáxias*, finalized a complete translation with the cooperation of Suzanne Jill Levine, and selections can be found online at a Canadian university website.[17]

I would like to share a document composed (in Portuguese) in Austin when Prof. Haroldo passed away. It's a sympathy letter sent on August 27, 2003:

> To Carmen and Ivan de Campos and Family: We the undersigned of the Department of Spanish and Portuguese of the University of Texas wish to convey our deepest condolences on the occasion of the passing of the great poet and critic—and good friend—Haroldo de Campos. Haroldo not only left friends and admirers among students and professors here in our Department, he also for several years contributed notably to the national and international projection of our activities in teaching and literary research. Our Department owed much to him and we still do, especially those of us who worked together with the dearly departed colleague, Haroldo de Campos. A collective embrace and friendship, signed.

Although I spent only one semester as Haroldo's student in that department, I can say with confidence that he remained with me forever, in memories and literary pages. Besides the articles I wrote with links to Haroldo, I published three books in the United States about Brazilian lyric, and all three bear the marks of the professor. The main thrust of *Masters of Contemporary Brazilian Song: MPB 1965–1985* is the poetry of song, and one of the key points of departure was the seminar on the baroque. The title of *Seven Faces: Brazilian Poetry since Modernism* alludes to Drummond's signature poem but signs of the master Haroldo are strong from the very concept of *modernismo* to the appreciation of his watershed essay on the "poema pos-utópico" (the post-utopian poem), which prepared us for the end of the millennium. More recently, *Brazil, Lyric, and the Americas* availed itself of Haroldo upon considering Sousândrade, Oswald, and North American statements, but above all in the case of the Latin American neo-baroque and the inter-American relationship with Octavio Paz. All this is reinforced whenever I speak with young poets who admire Haroldo the writer and the ambassador.

In conclusion, I would like to return to the theme of translation and memories of Austin. Another item I discovered in an old filing cabinet while preparing this paper was a large index card on which was written with a red Sharpie the rough draft of a translation of one of Haroldo's most representative concrete poems, "nascemorre." It was an attempt to create a compact version attentive to the combinations of letters and other geometric factors. If memory serves, I was asked in 1981 what I thought of the few English translations of Brazilian concrete poetry. Reconstructing the exchange, I dared to opine that within the principle of the "verbi-voco-visual ideogram" the translators favored excessively the verbi-, the semantic dimension, overlooking sonorous and technical aspects. A perfect example would be the rather literal version of "nascemorre" in *Concrete Poetry: A World View*, the most famous international anthology of the genre. I found realizations of my preferences for concision, parallelism, mirrorings, and so on, decades later in an internet post by a new doctor in comparative literature who had earlier done a master's thesis on Arnaldo Antunes.[18] I would have liked to see this in advance of completing a detailed article on the question of re-creating "nascemorre."[19] In this study, I discuss the even greater difficulty of translating *poesia concreta* and, nevertheless, the faith of the Brazilian concrete poets, superb translators, in *transcriação* (transcreation), and in *tradução-arte* (translation-art), providing all is done with due care. I discuss four extant versions of "nascemorre" in English, one a simple gloss and three attempts at translation per se: the one mentioned above, another rather literal one, and a final well-thought-out one that managed to lose a line. In sum, each one has its strong and weak points. What if, I propose in this paper-homage to Haroldo, one should generate a multiple translation? A four-handed composition, so to speak, one version for each triangle of the original, each favoring a particular aspect or two over other features. The result is two versions favoring the hypothetical semanteme with "if," the pronominal, and the impersonal, via nouns, not conjugated verbs. And two other versions based on, respectively, the phoneme */i/* and the grapheme *-e*. Finally, a combination of all four versions in one big poem with four equilaterally distributed members. Thus, one might grasp how much is going on in the original. I only wish I had thought of all this in 1981 to be able to share it live, austinatiously, with professor Haroldo de Campos in his *Austineia Desvairada*.

9

"Logopéia via Goethe via Christopher Middleton"

An Unknown Recording of Haroldo de Campos (Austin, 1981)

KENNETH DAVID JACKSON

In 1981, the Brazilian poet Haroldo de Campos (1929–2003) came to Austin with his wife, Carmen, and young son, Ivan, to spend spring semester at the University of Texas, a time that would prove to be one of his most creative. He had taught in Austin a decade earlier (the spring of 1970) and nourished affection for the department once visited by some of Latin America's most celebrated writers: Jorge Luis Borges, Cecília Meireles, and Clarice Lispector.[1] I worked with him a decade earlier in São Paulo, where he aided my thesis research on Oswald de Andrade. Once I joined the faculty of the University of Texas, I invited Haroldo for a lecture in April 1978; his spontaneous poem "Visão do Paraíso," composed during his flight to Austin on Braniff Airlines, was published in Spain in a limited edition, with my translation to English.[2] I was next successful in obtaining a nomination for Haroldo as Edward Laroque Tinker Visiting Professor. Haroldo was extremely active that semester in the spring of 1981: besides his seminars on Brazilian literature, he wrote the poems for

"Austineia Desvairada" (later published in *A educação dos cinco sentidos*, São Paulo: Brasiliense, 1985); organized the symposium "scribblevaganza" with the Dutch poet Hans Ten Berg and others; collaborated with Christopher Middleton (1926–2015), English poet and professor of German language and literature; and for several weeks in May received Emir Rodríguez Monegal, his former colleague from Yale University, where Haroldo had been visiting professor in 1978. It was during this semester that Haroldo translated "Blanco" by Octavio Paz in one marathon session, which he later described in conversation: "Tomei a mescalina de mim mesmo e passei a noite em claro traduzindo 'Blanco' de Octavio Paz." The translation was one of the high points of Haroldo's visits to the United States, enhanced by the red cowboy shirts, lone star buttons, and armadillo belt buckles that made up the Texan image of Haroldo de Campos. We spent a happy and creative semester in his company. In 2008, in preparation for a lecture at the Casa das Rosas in São Paulo, where Haroldo's literary archive is located, I was fortunate to recuperate an aural memoir of those times in a forgotten cassette recording.

Haroldo's collaboration with Christopher Middleton produced three important translations: the translation to Portuguese of Middleton's poem "Cabaret de la Canne"; a poem by Goethe, "Herbstgefuhl" (1755), previously translated into English by Middleton and based on that text into Portuguese by Haroldo; and Middleton's translation, with Norman Potter, of a fragment of Haroldo's novel *Galáxias*. Haroldo did maintain an intense level of activity and the joy of what he called "transcreation."

Two Poems and Their Translations

One of Haroldo's goals in transcreation was to find creative parallels in Portuguese for linguistic dimensions and components of the original. In Middleton's poem, we see moments in which Haroldo follows the original faithfully and others in which he makes the original language more synthetic. Near the beginning, notice how he handles the problem of the adjective "little" in English; his solution is to place the word ("exíguo") in parentheses. Although not present in the original, his solution solves the linguistic problem while maintaining the meaning.

He inverts "Glittering still, the flake of snow I flicked / From the collar of my coat when I came in" to "um floco de neve—brilho tranqüilo—que eu / recém-entrado, sacudi da gola do casaco," capturing very well the rhythm, sound, and alliteration in "o ritmo e o som," above all in "Flake/flicked." He reduces the phrase "When I came in" to "recém entrado," thus solving the problem of wordiness in English. For "his own slowly turning universe" he uses "giro lento," separating the expression from the noun "universo," more synthetically.

Certain solutions work out especially well, such as his translation of the phrase "Important smells." This phrase sounds ironic in English, unless one is addressing perfume salesmen, and "Odores relevantes" captures the irony as well as the uncommonness, while "repregam e flexionam" captures the sounds in "wrinkle and flex." For "mysterious names, numbers, and messages," his solution, "nomes, enigmas, números, mensagens," follows the alliterative sequence while adding another adjective, thus intensifying the pattern of vowels.

In other places Haroldo takes more liberties, not only with words but also with the meaning. For example, "There are places where people turn yellow, / Having nothing to eat" becomes "Há lugares de gente amarela, / sem nada para comer." Here the people are yellow, and the reader must be more imaginative, while in English the people simply turn yellow. The solution for "Broken roofs. Through holes the snow sifts" is "Telhados rotos. Neve que vaza," where Haroldo creates two strong independent images, as in the phrase "A Valois song," which becomes "Valois: um canto," using a juxtaposition rather than an adjective.

In the case of "The last vine still grew / A veiny green, very ancient," full of v's and e's, the solution, "cresce a última vinha, / um verde vasculado, vetusto, / a última vinha," is even stronger than the original. In the phrase "The emperor was Julian and Paris Egypt," Haroldo substitutes the "and" with a semicolon, making the phrase even more synthetic: "era Juliano o imperador; Paris, Egito." That curious word in English, "indispose," here applied to a cat, is usually used by upper-class or pretentious people. Here Haroldo captures the situation perfectly with "perturbar": "Não é o caso de perturbar o gato."

Finally, we notice certain "transcreative" solutions that show Haroldo's particular genius. By using "os dedos de um espírito entintam, em nossa íntima pele" for "The fingers of a spirit ink into our skins," his use of the verb "entintam" not only reinforces the sonorous alliteration but also maintains the unexpected use of "ink" as a verb. For "two rescued Fragonnards," Haroldo finds a poetic result, "resgata dois súbitos Fragonnards," where the surprising adjective "súbitos" enhances the sensation of sudden discovery.

"Herbstgefühl": Poem by Goethe

For Goethe's poem, translated to English by Middleton, Haroldo invents the title "Logopéia via Goethe via Christopher Middleton." His translation was eventually published in *O arco-iris branco* (Rio de Janeiro: Imago, 1997), but without the English version that served as its model. The theme here is the change of seasons, from summer to fall, with the approaching decadence and death of foliage. This is the first time that I ever heard Haroldo use the expression "tradução brasileira" for one of his translations, when the term "transcreation" was normally sufficient to describe his methods. Could it be that he found the solutions here to be more malleable, flexible, or freer, such that they deserved to be called a "tradução brasileira"? In any case, we have one more label to apply to Haroldo's work: "tradutor brasileiro."

Certainly, Haroldo changed the original, beginning by altering the sixteen lines and extending to his portmanteau invention "plenibrilha." Notice that the sole exclamation in the original, "Ach!"—while not retained in the English translation—becomes useful for a mischievous Haroldian alliterative pun: "E desses olhos onde amor—ah!—," a solution that could be understood orally as "onde amor há" (where love exists). With the closing "túmidas lágrimas," Haroldo returns to the original, but omitting the word "brimming" that had been added by Middleton. Although his translation is published, the poem was nonetheless forgotten for many years, without anyone knowing about or having access to the English translation that served as Haroldo's model in Austin in 1981. After remaining for twenty-nine years "in the drawer," this important recording has surfaced to help us understand the pleasure of translation in the creative method used by Haroldo de Campos and in hearing the voices of the poets. Let's listen now to the poets' reading of the texts.

Voice of Christopher Middleton:
"Cabaret de la Canne, January 1855, a poem by Christopher Middleton, read by Christopher Middleton."

CABARET DE LA CANNE, JANUARY 1855

Sir, I do not know your name,
Nor do you know mine. So we sit.
Briefly, at neighbouring tables, you
With your bottle, the cat on your knee,
I with my little glass.

In our sunken ship
The third table has been taken
By the fine man of darkness, whom
We do not see. Look, on the furrowed surface
Glittering still, the flake of snow I flicked
From the collar of my coat when I came in.

Each sits watching
The face of his own slowly turning
Universe. Particularly the cat
Has known how the heat

Comes and goes. Important smells
Wrinkle and flex into signatures, you know,
Writ small in snowflakes and the skeletons
Of leaves. Shuddering.
The fingers of a spirit ink into our skins
Mysterious names, numbers, and messages.

Ancient gutters
Accommodate the cat, providing
Fish, spare ribs, a scrap of lamplight;
Spilt milk to lap up, now and then.

There are places where people turn yellow,
Having nothing to eat. Cloacas, attics.
Broken roofs. Through holes the snow sifts.
A Valois song can be issuing, in another street,
From a little girl's lips
For a penny.

Mandolins, a lantern swaying, make it
Difficult to want less than a tree to dance with.
Do we suffer
Most because the bunched worms will hang
In the emptiness you are looking at, this
Dome of mine, bald, this bony cabin?

What is immortal
If not the injustice?

There was a room I lived in once,
I remember how the early light in it
Fell across two rescued Fragonnards.
There was a girl, nearly naked she was,
Tigers ran before her on a leash
And a little donkey woke us, braying,
Or a barge trumpet's echo off the river.

Like a swift in his globe of crisp mud
I hung between sleep and waking
And heard the straw speak in my thin
Mattress. Look, here it is, another face

Of that same
Towering light, again
In this bit of a rainbow, at its peril
Afloat in eau-de-vie:
I drink it for the dream that spills
Into life.

They tore it down, it was an old house.
They did not tear down
The other room, which, if you follow me,
We put there, suspending it
Outside any space that iron balls
Can shatter.

In that room the last vine still grew,
A veiny green, very ancient.
The last vine, first planted when
The emperor was Julian and Paris Egypt.
From that vine,
Yes from it you might see
A light as from the original stars unfolded
And flew as it pleased, to vary
As it touched the featured walls through
Twelve emotions. With snaky lines
It marbled the stones and old chairs
We had broken by leaning back to laugh.
To eye the stones was to feel a flow
Of female warmths and hear the goddess,—
Moan and shriek of the sistron in her fingers.

What can you be thinking?
No, do not indispose the cat.[3]

Voice of Haroldo de Campos:
"Poem by Christopher Middleton, translated into Portuguese by Haroldo de Campos and read by the translator."

CABARET DE LA CANNE, JANEIRO 1855
Senhor, não sei seu nome, nem
o senhor sabe o meu. Assim nos
sentamos, rápidos, mesas vizinhas, você

com sua garrafa, o gato nos joelhos,
eu com meu copo
(exíguo).

Nesse nosso navio náufrago
a mesa três foi tomada
pelo sutil homem da treva, que
não enxergamos. Veja, no tampo rugoso,
um floco de neve—brilho tranqüilo—que eu,
recém-entrado, sacudi da gola do casaco.

Cada qual assentado contempla
a face do seu próprio—giro lento—
universo. O gato em
particular sabe quando o fogo
aquenta ou some. Odores relevantes
repregam ou flexionam—você sabe—
assinaturas, miúda inscrição
em flocos de neve ou esqueletos
de folhas. Estremecendo
os dedos de um espírito entintam, em nossa
íntima pele, nomes, enigmas, números,
mensagens.

Esgotos ancestrais
acomodam o gato, providenciam
peixe, costelas poupadas, uma lasca de luz;
leite entornado, lambidas, de quando em
quando.

Há lugares de gente amarela,
sem nada para comer. Cloacas, águas-
furtadas. Telhados rotos. Neve que vaza.

Valois: um canto pode estar surgindo,
numa outra rua, nos lábios de uma criança,
por um mínimo vintém.

Mandolinas, balanço de lanterna, difícil
desejar menos que uma árvore
para esta dança. Será que sofremos,
mais do que tudo, pelo cacho de vermes, que

há de restar, pênsil,
nesse oco, para onde você olha, agora, esta
minha cúspide calva, domo, cabina de ossos?

Imortal? O que é senão a injustiça?

Houve um quarto onde outrora eu vivi;
lembro-me como a primeira luz, que incide
nele, resgata dois súbitos Fragonards.
Havia uma jovem, quase nua,
precedida por um salto de tigres,
e um burrico nos acordou, zurrando,
ou uma buzina de barca, rio acima, o eco.

Andorinha em seu globo de barro crespo,
oscilei entre sono e vigília,
e ouvi a fala da palha em minha cama
rasa. Olhe, eis aí, uma outra face
da mesma luz em torre, outra
vez nesta nesga de íris, perigosamente
à tona da eau-de-vie;
sorvo-a: deságua sonho na vida.

Derrubaram-na, era uma casa velha.
Não derrubaram o outro quarto,
o qual, se você me seguir,
ubicaremos ali, suspenso,
além de qualquer espaço que bolas de ferro,
maciças, possam rebentar.

Nesse quarto cresce a última vinha,
um verde vasculado, vetusto,
a última vinha, plantada quando
era Juliano o Imperador; Paris, Egito.
Dessa vinha,
sim, dela você veria
uma luz como de estrelas primeiras
despontar, irradiar-se, vária, cambiando
ao tocar o desenho das paredes, doze
diferentes emoções. Traço serpentino
marmorando pedras e velhas cadeiras
quebradas quando rindo

nos estirávamos para trás.
O olho na pedra sente uma febre
femínea, fluente, e ouve a deusa: o grito
lastimoso do sistro entre seus dedos.

Você, no que estará pensando agora?
Não, não é o caso de perturbar o gato.
(Austin, 1981, unpublished translation)

Voice of Christopher Middleton:
"This is a curious poem by Goethe written in 1775. First, I'll read the German, then my English translation."

HERBSTGEFÜHL (JOHANN WOLFGANG VON GOETHE)
Fetter grüne, du Laub,
Am Rebengelander
Hier mein Fenster herauf!
Gedrängter quellet,
Zwillingsbeeren, und reifet
Schneller und glänzend voller!
Euch brütet der Mutter Sonne
Scheideblick, euch umsäuselt
Des holden Himmels
Fruchtende Fülle:
Euch kühlet des Mondes
Freundlicher Zauberhauch,
Und euch betauen, ach!
Aus diesen Augen
Der ewig belebenden Liebe
Vollschwellende Tränen.

AUTUMN FEELING (1775)
More fatly greening climb
The trellis, you, vine leaf
Up to my window!
Gush, denser, berries
Twin, and ripen
Shining fuller, faster!
Last gaze of sun
Broods you, maternal:
Of tender sky the fruiting
Fullness wafts around you:

Cooled you are, by the moon
Magic, a friendly breath,
And from these eyes,
Of ever quickening Love, ah,
Upon you falls a dew, the tumid
Brimming tears.[4]

Voice of Haroldo de Campos:
"Portuguese translation of the same text under the title *Logopéia via Goethe via Christopher Middleton*. Tradução brasileira do mesmo poema sob o título *Logopéia via Goethe via Christopher Middleton*, por Haroldo de Campos."

LOGOPÉIA VIA GOETHE VIA CHRISTOPHER MIDDLETON
Gordura verde, tu
folhagem e treliça, aqui,
subindo a videira ao meu
balcão!

Tufa, amadura, mais
denso ainda colar
de bagas geminadas, pleni-
brilha!

Te incuba o sol—mãe
sol—olho estremoso circum-
zumbe a teu redor o pleno
pulso frutal do
amável céu.

Te esfria a lua—sopro
cordial, magia.

E desses olhos onde amor—ah!—
semprevive sempre-
demora e mais, cai sobre ti agora
o orvalho: túmidas
lágrimas.[5]

10

Meeting in Austin

BENEDITO NUNES

At the beginning of 1981, some visiting professors in the Brazilian Literature program at the University of Texas in Austin found us, me and Haroldo de Campos, under the cold sky of an indecisive Texas winter. I visited him in the evening; he was the first tenant of the apartment, and already familiar with its water bugs and remained indifferent to these "legionnaire cockroaches" that populated the routine of Campos's "Austinéia Desvairada." I read one or two chapters to Haroldo, part of an in-progress book called the *Paisagem para a poética (Filosofia e poesia em Heidegger)*, where I referred to the Heideggarian concepts of language and poetry based in part on "Aus einem Gespräch von der Sprache" (Of a Conversation with Language), a work with which Haroldo was very familiar. Our conversation was peppered with some small pauses in order to read, and in the years since I have remembered Haroldo's proposition of the two of us having a conversation one day that was deeply interconnected, a dialogue within a dialogue, concentric or eccentric to his work.

If that proposition was never realized, it is down to my false expectations as I was waiting for some essayistic prose from my interlocutor. Today, I understand that he took our discussion to heart immediately, right there in Austin, but not in conversation or in prose. I didn't realize it at the time. He did so through poetry in "Aisthesis, Kharis: Iki—Koan (Heideggerean poetics for Benedito Nunes)," a poem from his "Austinéia Desvairada," included in *A educaçao dos cinco sentidos* (1985).

The reflex to unpack how I came close to the work of Haroldo de Campos—a note that is perhaps impertinent, laden with the generality that many philosophical explanations often have on poetic texts—is a tardy response to the dialogue that led to the creation of that poem-commentary by Haroldo.

se heidegger tivesse olhado
para o ideograma
enquanto escutava o discípulo
japonês
(como pound olhou para *ming* 明 sollua
com o olho cubista de gaudier-brzeska
depois de dar ouvido a fenollosa)
teria visto que a cerejeira cereja *koto ba* 言葉
das ding dingt
florchameja
no espaço indecidível
da palavra
iki[1]

This poem, which is exemplary of the work of Haroldo de Campos in more than one way (as we will see) and delineating the interlocutory situation of Heideggerean writing, also synthesizes the complex problematic associated with language traced on the page. The pretext that I refer to is, within the hypothetical enunciation articulated in its thirteen verses, the subsequent weakness I showed in understanding "iki," in comprehending this word that escaped me as I had not looked at the respective ideogram in the work while I listened to the disciple discuss the meaning of that word in our original dialogue in Austin. If I had looked, I would have seen that the "cerejeira cereja" (cherry tree cherries)—*koto ba*. And I did not look, because I favored hearing and listening over seeing as the adopted attitude when it came to language. All of Heidegger's philosophy, which in its last stage was a rejection of philosophy in the name of a hermeneutics of language and an interpretation of the being as the only object of thought, was effectively based on listening, on a hearing of the written word of the texts of poets and philosophers.

The interlocutory situation in "Aus einem Gespräch von der Sprache—Zwischen einem Japaner und einem Fragenden" (A Conversation of Language: Between a Japanese and an Inquisitor), collected in *Unterwegs zur Sprache* (1959), refers to the dialogue between Heidegger and Professor Tezuka, from the Imperial University of Tokyo. Heidegger visited him in the 1950s, one of the last disciples of the German philosopher. Count Shuzo Kuki, by then dead, and Tanabé were among the others who had been close to him, back before the publication of *Sein und Zeit* (1927) when he was still working as an assistant at the seminars of Edmund Husserl. That lineage of students in the Land of the Rising Sun justified the visit in the 1950s; as Heidegger remembered it, his amicable debate that he once had with Count Kuki about the applicability of European aesthetics to Japanese art, which the latter postulated, was the motivation behind his conversation with Tezuka. According to the inquisitor, in an age of the globalization of ideas and philosophy, which exported the way of life in the industrial society all over the world, the Japanese way of being was endangered. That same spirit also represented the effect of European languages across the world that would prevent Heidegger from understanding the meaning of *iki* in that distant moment back in the 1920s. It was familiar to the old Japanese master who sought to apply aesthetics—after a phenomenological rethinking—to the study of art in his country. That earlier interaction guided the coming together of these two professors in the 1950s.

All the complex, ambiguous, and often misjudged problematics of Heidegger's philosophy—after the analysis of Dasein—were compressed in this interaction. Both interlocutors were driven by the thrill of contouring and deviating and by the conceptual structures that confined them in culturally static worlds under the safeguard of the "destructions" encompassed by Metaphysics and Aesthetics. There was a step back toward the being, the forgotten origin, and also the beginning of a new way of thinking—of an essentially poetic thinking, neither representational nor propositional, and free of the homogenous dominance of logic and grammatical categorizations. Already tangible, but ineffective, in its force and in that sense still to come, this poetic thinking (*dichtend Denken*), diffuse yet profuse and rooted at once in the poesis of language and in the impulse of the word behind the being, makes both a poetic thinking and a poetry of thinking compatible and possible in the oscillating philosophical formulations. Fundamental speech of language, far from the expression of existences, is always talking to us, principally in the texts of poet-philosophers and in those of poets of poetry (minus, it would seem, the explicit philosophy), an ongoing correspondence between man and being.

Following that gesture of correspondence, the two interlocutors could understand that, for the Japanese, the meaning of "Iki" (something close to "grace"), like the Greek "Kharis," is that the truth within art is independent of Aesthetics. "Koto ba"—petals of flowers originated by the joyous glory of grace—is a term that in Japanese and for Tezuka refers to language but is, to Heidegger, the truth of language, irrespective of linguistic nuance and incompatible with the language of metaphysics that gave us *Sprache*—speech.

Before the apophantic, and following Marc Richir's suggestion, the truth about the root of poetics is what language says by showing or what it shows by saying. It is there that we see the poetry of thought through hermeneutics and that only shows itself in essential speech to those who know how to hear it when they hear the word.

The first significant piece of Haroldo de Campos's poem is the subtle critique of the poetry of thought formulated in that way, in which he implicates the hypothesis of the failure of the philosopher in understanding the word "Iki." Our interlocutor has incessantly seen what could be called a poetry of thought, in the form of either his own "free verse, fecund" or his galactic verse-prose as well as in the transplanting of creation in a foreign language through translation. Why, then, the criticism on his part? A brief review of the two paths of the meditative practice executed by Heidegger as a hermeneutic of language might serve as a clarification.

The first path is the "renovated listening" of the Greek word in the pre-Socratics to direct them toward inaugural thought, right next to the source of origin and that later metaphysics overcame. The second is directed toward an interpretation of his preferred poets—from Holderlin to Rilke, from Stefan George to Trakl—and is also a listening to their texts as a means of letting the language speak. They both presuppose the instauration of being by language. Following the line of thought developed, above all, in the essays *Unterwegs zur Sprache*, likewise they presuppose a cyclical foundation: language establishes the being, but it is the plea of that same being that underwrites language and puts us into dialogue with it. On the other hand, this not-exclusively-inter-human dialogue is dependent on that same plea, of which the poet is the "messenger." Thus, the dialogic access that the philosopher enjoys to the essence of language, realized as listened-to speech without any other mediation besides the listening to the being that provokes the same effort of listening to texts, dispenses the character of the word symbol.

That is where the restraint of Haroldo comes in, a poet and essayist who highlighted the visibility, corporeality, and spatiality of the poetic word as symbol. Heidegger did not even look at the ideogram, a term barely mentioned in passing in the conversation between the two professors. If he could have looked with the eye of someone who knows how to look—in this case Tezuka's eye, who limited himself to stated words without, at least, informing Heidegger about the limitations of such an approach—he would have had an epiphany about the flesh of pictographic symbols; in other words, that the "cerejeira cereja" (cherry tree cherries) is something that one does not get by only listening to the word being spoken. And he would have perceived yet more, given that the ideogram functions through metaphor "florchameja" (flowerflickering), a true solo of thought made into poetry or of the poetry of thought.

In consonance with that notation, the poem we are considering shows us a sensitive, symbolic charge. It is from there that, in Haroldo's work, a poetry of thought flowers that has its roots in metaphor. From the verbal topsoil of meaning to the subsoil of rhythmic-semantic components, the chords of sound and feeling, and the revelation of the graphicality of words on the page. "Meisterludi ensinou-lhe o peso das vogais / Plúvia e dilúvio / sombra e umbra / penumbra" (from "Ciropédia ou a Educação do Príncipe"). It taught the poet to descend to the pre-categorized and to the pre-reflexive level, to the inference and to the limbo of thought oscillating between language and word, between semiotic and semantic: what Giorgio Agamben called the infancy of language.

Having rejected the duality of meaning and the signifier as if a metaphysical shadow case over being, Heidegger put metaphor under the microscope for the same reason: a retort to the separation of the felt and the nonfelt as two self-sufficient domains (as he wrote in *Der Satz vom Grund* in 1957). When he says that "the metaphorical only exists within the metaphysical," he concedes too much to metaphysics—forgetting everything that pre-Socratic thought owes to metaphor—and too little to metaphor. It is as though he forgot that he is the very act of language, its energy (to follow Humboldt) or the beginning of their game (to follow Wittgenstein). It is fitting, then, that it was this same word (and one of the more eminent ones of later Heideggerean thought), "game," that allowed him to bring together the likenesses of the essence of being in one term: *Zeit-Spiel-Raum* (free play of time-space or time-play-space). Like one big metaphor, it is the word of the poet from the same family as many other constellate figures that are, at once, limited concepts of the meditation of the philosopher and tropes of Heidegger's very personal philosophical style to whose orbit of poetic confluence belongs the verbalization of nouns: *Die Welt weltet* (the world worlds), *Die Zeit zeitigt* (time times), and *Ding dingt* (the thing things). As motioned by Henri Meschonnic, Heidegger is a poetic adventure touched down in Germany whose commentaries of poems are made of parapoems. Parapoetics are commentaries of the philosopher on poetry, commenting on the poem with a poem. If he were to deny the symbolic constitution of the language he would, ipso facto, deny the possibility of metalanguage, and from there we see the difficulty for the meditative practice of the philosopher to make language speak (*zum Wort kommt*). At this hermeneutic limit, one either returns to the concept (and thus the reflexive element, which Heidegger wants to avoid with metalanguage) or concedes the initiative to words, a passage to Mallarmé and from philosophy to poetry.

Now we can perceive that the ninth verse of "Aisthesis, Kharis: Iki" is an ironic quotation of the tautological poetics of *Das Ding dingt*, an attempt at the topology of being. The thing things like the cherry tree cherries like the flower flickers. The irony of the citation in this Heideggerean poetics makes apparent that Heidegger arrived at the auricular style of his last philosophy—more Hebrew than Greek, as Marlène Zarader observes in *La Dette Impenseé*—with *Das Ding dingt*, an analogous result that had also led to a style of poetry measured by its cubist visuality and by Chinese intelligence.

(como pound olhou para *ming* 明 sollua
com o olho cubista de gaudier-brzeska
depois de dar ouvido a fenollosa)[2]

In this progression, Haroldo de Campos's poetic glossary is subtly amplified to include one of the main themes of "Of a Conversation with Language," the Heidegger text that was part of my work-in-progress that I read to Haroldo in Austin: the danger of decharacterizing the culture of the Far East as a result of the planetary expansion of the technical, making—for example, and as Tezuka suggested—Kurosawa's *Rashomon* more Western than Eastern. The two professors, Heidegger and Tezuka, forgot to consider the counterpart of this process that began in the nineteenth century with the rejection of Far Eastern intellectual and spiritual culture in European culture, as channeled by Pound and Fenollosa for poetry in the time of their modernity.

Taking all that into account, if we now think about the title of Haroldo's poem ("Aisthesis, Kharis: Iki"), we can see that the irony of his commentary extends to the irony of history: the two Greek matrices (the profane "Aisthesis" and the sacred "Kharis") correspond with the "Iki" that synthesizes the two terms. Taking ourselves out of the scope of the poem, that correspondence signals the historical reach of those matrices. The last note on the exemplarity of the verses we have looked at comes with the title, an emblem of the proximity between poetry and thought or, if you will, between poetry and philosophy. "To poem and to think mutually need each other . . ." (Dichten und denken brauchen einander . . .). We can add that they need each other even more after philosophy reached its end point, the summit of its metaphysical possibilities, and after universal poetry (in the sense of the mixing of genres and forms of expression, the prosaic and the poetic to which Friedrich Schlegel referred) came to conjugate poetic styles and inheritances from the past.

But in Haroldo de Campos, the proximity between poetry and thought (as his Heideggerean poetics suggest) is established by the reflex introduced in the midst of the language game, which Heidegger never allowed. Thus, one can conclude that in the work of my interlocutor in Austin and after (and in constant dialogue with other thinker-poets like Heraclitus and Al-Ghazali and with poet-thinkers such as Dante, Goethe, and Leopardi), the poetry of thought—as much in creation as in re-creative translation—is complemented by the thought of poetry historically and critically considered.

Part III

Poems

11

Three Variations on Octavio Paz's "Blanco" and Fifteen Antiphonals for Haroldo de Campos, with a Note on Translation, Transcreation, and Othering

JEROME ROTHENBERG

BLANCO I: A VARIATION IN SEVEN SEGMENTS FOR OCTAVIO PAZ

1. white as the land looks | the vultures | white also | circle above | each one a soul | glows white | on horizon | or on page

2. the land is the land | it is white | thunderheads cover it | drumbeats | joining the land | & the sky

3. sky receptive to thunder | drumbeats to sky | white to colors | faces to eyes | sand turning white | like the sky

4. green is also | a color | like flesh | stung by thorns | my body | or yours | sparks a rage | like a drumbeat | violent | mineral | white

5. uproots trees | marks the land | like a body | shattered by lightning | the word | once proclaimed | white turns yellow

6. those who beat | on a waterdrum | spines tightly pressed | to a wall | & the drumbeat | spreads violet ash | on the sky | a sun glowing white

7. language | a desert | pink everywhere | seeds in your mouth | like white crows | & more drumbeats | a flute | turns everything white

BLANCO 2: A VARIATION IN FIVE SEGMENTS FOR OCTAVIO PAZ

1. A clarity | of all the senses | lingers | leaving on the mouth & face | a white precipitation | sculptures crystal-thin | blank space | translucid whirlpools

2. Is it a pilgrimage | that brings us | dancing in a ring | into a forest | where our thoughts | are white | the only signs | our steps | that break the silence

3. Green would be better | a slim defile | through which we pass | an archipelago | the shadow of a syllable | a white reflection

4. Is it red | or is it blue | this dazzlement | that blinds us | numbers | dancing in the void | like *things* | a final clarity | no longer white

5. Thoughts fade | winds cease | forgetfulness erases truth | there is a deeper music in the words we speak | yellow isn't white | & amethyst | is just a color

BLANCO 3: A VARIATION IN NINE SEGMENTS FOR OCTAVIO PAZ

1. Presentiment & penumbra | hide the river | where the sand | still white | buries a palm | a pike emerging | skewers our vowels | as we speak

2. Blood fills the mouth | the chest counts anxious minutes | as the dead might | undulations | of a copper lamp | high overhead | casting a shadow

3. Transparency in daylight | where a river | seeks a river | poles apart | the consonants feel heavy | water vanishes | the drought starts up

4. The Spanish centuries | remain anonymous | against my forehead | silt | obscures a castle | coal burns yellow | patience ends | a white confusion | covers all

5. What does the vase hold? | blood & bones | not flowers | the sad reality of words | a language of atonement | silences & syllables | white as this dust

6. No further clarity | than this | no histories or hieroglyphs | to guide us | dunes & water all around | conspiracies of light | absent survivors

7. White bones | appeasement hard to find | or patience | when we climb the ladder | mineshafts open up | below | a red hand beckons

8. His source is Mexico | his language set apart from | all the others | white on white

9. pulsebeat quickens | on the playing card he holds | a foliage unfolds for him | a language no one reads | a river rife with whitecaps | rolling by

15 ANTIPHONALS: FOR HAROLDO DE CAMPOS

burnt by
        asthma

churn'd
        miasma

•

a blind
        nail
        oiling
sun's
        axis

a kind
        whale
        spoiling
nun's
        praxis

•

the malice
        of the
        mastery

the chalice
        of her
        chastity

•

from muse
        to medusa
        all hot

when recused
the accuser
will rot

•

mirrormoon
in the mirage

silverspoon
for persiflage

•

the crux
of the
incredible

the flux
of the
inedible

•

the fire
became
water
the water
a body of
vapor

the tiger
proclaimed
slaughter
the slaughter
modified
nature

•

weary
weary
weary
and a fury

dreary
dreary

dreary
in missouri

•

mirror
of the self
mature

silver
on my shelf
secure

•

Sitar
of the tongue,
how does one
hear?

Guitar
once unstrung
is never
clear

•

Unlike
the bird
according to
nature
but as
a god

Hiding
his word
under their
strictures
rebuff'd
with a nod

•

in front
of a
greater king
a king

lesser
great

unsung
who will
later sing
will more
sing
still late

•

minute
commentaries

hirsute
dromedaries

•

secure a cut
a sure shot
on the bull's eye

skewer a cunt
the whore hot
on the driveby

•

against
the unflinching
light
the eye
turns
emerald

beneath
the diminished
night
the sky
burns
unheralded

A Note of the Preceding: Translation, Transcreation, and Othering

1.

The crux of the matter here was Haroldo de Campos's theory and practice of *transcreation*, something that was very much on my mind since our first meetings in Europe nearly two decades ago.[1] For me—and I believe for Haroldo as well—this brought up the question of my own practice with translation in *Technicians of the Sacred* (1968) and beyond, as well as the still larger dimension of what I had come to call "othering" and, more narrowly, "total translation." Like him I came more and more to think of translation as the foundation for the larger part of what I and others had been practicing as poetry—at least that our treating it as such raised some productive questions about the nature of poetry and of language overall. (This was also at the heart of the Noigandres experiment, for which Haroldo of course was one of the prime movers.) And this centrality of translation was hammered home as well by Octavio Paz, so that the conjunction of Campos and Paz in the present gathering made translation, transcreation, and othering the dominant themes for me as I approached it. For this, of course, Octavio's "Blanco" and Haroldo's transcreation thereof were the twin works open for our consideration.

My strategy here was to turn, as Haroldo had before me, to the original "Blanco," so as to further the earlier act of transcreation with a transcreative work of my own. I looked in doing so to a form of othering that I had begun to practice two decades before—in a series of poems, "The Lorca Variations," derived from the vocabulary of my own translations of García Lorca's early *Suites*. In those I systematically used all of Lorca's nouns (in my English translation) as nuclei from which to compose new poems. Moving from poem to poem I arranged the translated nouns in four or five columns and proceeded to link the words in something like reverse order, with results like the following, both Lorca and not Lorca, both mine and not mine:

THE LORCA VARIATIONS XV
"Water Jets"

1
If death once had a face
the water from this water jet
has wiped it out,
the August air has left no trace of it,
like other fountains
or other faces from your home town
that the sunlight & the water jet

drive from your room.
Things leave our eyes no boundaries here
other than dreams, no dreams
still precious to your heart,
its carved interior shot through with corners,
into which a grapevine grows,
fed by the water jet your fingers
once turned on, made it a place of clouds,
the perfect death's head still inside it,
& that a water jet wipes out.

2
It's night.
In the garden our hearts have turned blue.
A maid opens the water jet, lets water & roses spill out.
A century passes.
Pianos circle the earth, dark swords slice arteries.
No dust on your windows, just blood.
In the garden four gay caballeros trade swords.
A cloud breaks apart & starts quaking.
It's night.

2.

If the "Blanco" variations published here were my homage to Paz, in the case of Haroldo de Campos I brought forward a series of poems composed several years before and displaying a quite different form of othering. That series, which I called "Antiphonals" for obvious reasons, was part of a commission from Francesco Conz, a great collector and publisher of Fluxus and other avant-garde art and poetry, for poems to be written by hand on a series of large colored photo portraits of Haroldo. As my contribution to what was conceived as a group tribute, I took phrases and lines from English translations of Haroldo's poetry and responded to them with loosely rhymed soundings of my own. I then handwrote the poems pair by pair onto a black left margin on each of the photographs. In the typographical version above, Haroldo's words appear in italics, while mine are shown in roman type. For me at least, the resultant work has the feel of translation/transcreation—as still another instance of othering.

All of this is of course not unfamiliar to other poets and is part of what we mean when we speak not only of translation as such but of related procedures such as collage and appropriation. I am willing enough to extend all of these techniques so as to consider the consequences of viewing all our works (even the most "original" and "self expressive" ones) as aspects of such a deeply human procedure. Language is and has always been an aspect of our work in common, and there is a sense here, as I have stated often before, in which all translation and all of its related acts involve a kind of implicit collaboration—at least in the mind of the translator. I am very much aware of this, however one-sided it may often seem, and I have sometimes let myself believe that all our writing, all our poetry, is an activity shared by all who are the users and makers of our common language. This idea of a communally driven poetry—of the poem, however individual or unique, as simultaneously what Pound called "a tale of the tribe"—has held my attention even when I felt it to be false. In a world in which that kind of unity is again under fire, I would continue thinking in those terms, wherever it may take me.

12

Poems

ANTONIO CICERO

IGNORANT SKY

The well-built house has fallen to the ground.
There is no God among us anymore.
Now bay leaves wither, prophets are a bore
And not a single new spring has been found.
So you make a cockpit out of your bedroom
And opening electronic windows up
You scan the universe for kicks, and zoom
A distant face to get a fake close up;
And yet when everything's quite like a lie
And only what is terrible seems true
You find within your heart a strange devotion
Toward that star against an ignorant sky:
You know its shimmering artificial blue
Has been delivered by the deepest ocean.[1]

FALAR E DIZER

para Waly Salomão

Não é possível que portentos não tenham ocorrido
Ou visões ominosas e graves profecias
Quando nasci.
Então nasce o chamado
Herdeiro das superfícies e das profundezas então
Desponta o sol
E não estremunha aterrado o mundo?
Assim à idade da razão
Vazei os olhos cegos dos arúspices e,
Fazendo rasos seus templos devolutos,
Desde então eu designo no universo vão
As coisas e as palavras plenas.
Só
Com elas
Recôndito e radiante ao sopro dos tempos
Falo e digo
Dito e decoro
O caos arreganhado a receber-me incontinente.

SPEAKING AND SAYING

to Waly Salomão

It cannot be that no portent took place
Or ominous visions and grave prophecies
When I was born.
Then the so-called heir
Of surfaces and depths is born then
The sun appears
And is not the world startled from slumber in terror?
Thus in the age of reason
I ripped out the blind soothsayer's eyes and,
Laying flat their emptied temples,
Since then I designate in the vain universe
Things and words replete.
Alone
With them
Recondite and radiant in the breath of time
My speaking and saying
Dictating with decorum
The snarling chaos to receive me forthwith.[2]

LOGRADOR

Você habita o próprio centro
de um coração que já foi meu.
Por dentro torço pra que dentro
em pouco lá só more eu.

Livre de todos os negócios
e vícios que advêm de amar
lá seja o centro de alguns ócios
que escolherei por cultivar.

E pra que os sócios vis do amor,
rancor, dor, ódio, solidão,
não mais consumam meu vigor,

amado e amor banir-se-ão
do centro rumo a um logrador
subúrbio desse coração.

LOGRADOR

You inhabit the very heart
of a heart that once was mine
Deep down, I applaud the near future
when I alone live there;

free from the negotiations
and vices that come of loving
there should lie the center of more than one indolence
I shall choose to cultivate

and so that the vile associates of love,
spite, pain, hatred, solitude
no longer drain my vigor,

loved one and love shall be banished
from the center towards the swindling
suburbs of this heart.[3]

GUARDAR

Guardar uma coisa não é escondê-la ou trancá-la. Em cofre não se guarda coisa alguma. Em cofre perde-se a coisa à vista.
Guardar uma coisa é olhá-la, fitá-la, mirá-la por admirá-la, isto é, iluminá-la ou ser por ela iluminado.
Guardar uma coisa é vigiá-la, isto é, fazer vigília por ela, isto é, velar por ela, isto é, estar acordado por ela, isto é, estar por ela ou ser por ela.
Por isso melhor se guarda o vôo de um pássaro
Do que pássaros sem vôos.
Por isso se escreve, por isso se diz, por isso se publica, por isso se declara e declama um poema:
Para guardá-lo:
Para que ele, por sua vez, guarde o que guarda:
Guarde o que quer que guarda um poema:
Por isso o lance do poema:
Por guardar-se o que se quer guardar.

KEEPING

To keep something is not to conceal it or to leave it under lock and key.
Nothing is meant to be kept in coffers.
Offers in safes are lost from sight.
To keep something is to look at it, to look after it, to look up to it.
To keep something is to guard it and to regard it, to illuminate it and to be illuminated by it.
To keep something is to tend it, to attend to it, to watch over it, to keep a vigil for it, to stay awake for it, to be there for it, to be for it.
That's why one better keeps the flight of a bird
Than birds without flights.
That's why one writes, one speaks, one publishes,
That's why one declares and declaims a poem:
To keep it;
So that it may, in turn, keep whatever it keeps,
whatever a poem keeps:
Such is the lot of poems:
to keep whatever will be kept.[4]

SEGUNDO A TRADIÇÃO

O grande bem não nos é nunca dado
e foste já furtado do segundo:
O resto é afogar-te com o amado
na líquida volúpia de um segundo.

A SECOND TRADITION

What's best of all you never would discover;
Already you've been stolen from the second.
What's left for you but drowning with your lover,
In the voluptuous liquids of a second?[5]

O PAÍS DAS MARAVILHAS

Não se entra no país das maravilhas
pois ele fica do lado de fora,
não do lado de dentro. Se há saídas
que dão nele, estão certamente à orla
iridescente do meu pensamento,
jamais no centro vago do meu eu.
E se me entrego às imagens do espelho
ou da água, tendo no fundo o céu,
não pensem que me apaixonei por mim.
Não: bom é ver-se no espaço diáfano
do mundo, coisa entre coisas que há
no lume do espelho, fora de si:
peixe entre peixes, pássaro entre pássaros,
um dia passo inteiro para lá.[6]

THE WONDROUS LAND

There is no entry to the wondrous land
for it remains without and not within.
And if there be some exits close at hand
they're surely on the iridescent fringe
of each and every thought of mine revealed,
but never at the center of my soul.
And should I to the mirror's image yield
or to the water's, where the sky's so close,
don't think I'm captivated by myself.
Oh no! It's good to see oneself wherein
space is diaphanous and each thing shines
between the mirror's edge, outside its self;
a bird amid the birds and fish amid fish,
one day I'll slide completely to that side.[7]

13

Waves of Absence

KEIJIRO SUGA

1
That there are things that cannot be written
Was the most important teaching incorporated in words
We attempt to add something faraway to our experience
But our distance and ignorance will not change
That there are things that should not be put into words
Was the most modest vow of words
Drops of rain cannot challenge the sun
Grains of sand cannot beat the wind
In the same way words, as drops of rain, grains of sand,
Would accept evaporation, begin flying uncontrollably
Even so, there may be insects who quench their thirst with these drops of rain
And cling to these minute grains of sand
We are the bugs, so small, all of us are the bugs, so transient
Caught by the limits of our small bodies and sense organs
Never talking about the world, we live on
Beaten by the light and rain of the world

2
In the town where people have disappeared
On the wasteland where the town has disappeared
In this vast area littered with rubbles

A dog is running, on its self-assigned mission of patrol
What the dog is aiming at is connecting heat in surviving lives
He tries to connect somebody breathing and somebody blinking
And make them talk using unknown words
But he does not meet anybody
He stops once in a while, listens carefully, sniffs scents
And starts running again, in the town where dwelling has been cancelled
Running, the dog takes off its fur
He thinks of putting it on someone to warm up the person
Then he stops and lets his hot urine gush out
He is trying to mark his smell and life on the spot
Wondering where all the people have gone
The naked dog, out of his fur and now covered with blood, is silently running

3
"The Eyes see more than the Heart knows" (William Blake)
I've seen things that the heart cannot bear to know
Memories
What is projected on the clouds fringed with the color of corns
Are all the yesterdays up until yesterday
Nothing is lost up there
And nothing will be lost
Thanks to all the plants and animals that have dedicated their lives
The chronicle of this land has been written
Then when we turn our gaze from the clouds to the land
Look, mud from ten thousand years ago is exposed here
An ancient school of fish, chased by the absence of water, leaped
Their traces were then left on the mud
Hieroglyphs of history to us
Then after a while the letters started swimming once again
But the clouds dutifully remember our hearts

4
Under the cold spring sky, crisp and blue,
A white dove is walking on the white sand
In the sunlight, she shines in pure white
In the shadow, she changes her color and looks pitch black
Without intentions, without thoughts
But the way she walks, as if blinking
Is something that could be called her view of life and death
How does she set her cardinal point?

The white dove wanders between light and shadow
The white dove encourages transposition every time she walks
The white dove does not tell the reason of her errant walk
She would, she will, accept everything just as it is
Even if the land's water was swallowed by the sea
Even if the lava from the volcano flowed on the land
Even if a fallen meteor opened a hole in the ground
But me, I would cry, hitting the ground with a stone

5
The cows do not dare go out of this fence
They are not afraid of the wind's growl, not scared of the sea's roar
It is just that the humans they know are no longer there
So they feel nervous and stay put
Nearby, the marshes have thoroughly vanished
The migratory birds have lost their destination
In the town, all shops and temples are gone
And the cats go on wandering more than ever
On the hills, the horses are running around blowing breaths of fire
And the pigs have gained wings and are flying low in groups
The raccoons and weasels have made their mass exodus
Raptores and reptiles have not been sighted for a long time
Only the cows would not leave this place
Since they do not have appetite anymore, imaginary rumination is enough
Will the faces of familiar people not return the very next day?
The haggard cows are waiting fixedly for a hundred years already

6
Poetry is all about transcending time
Even more than music that's reproducible after five hundred years
Poetry sounds and depicts the same even in a different time and place
However different the reader and the meaning may be
Poetry, the patterns that appear on the sea surface of language,
Is handed over in the same shape
Because being the same is the only definition of poetry
Poetry is written over time
It may or may not be received
Poetry in itself is not prayer
But prayer attends poetry and embraces it
Poetry, the shape of words, does not have any physical power
Even so, when we, the Earth Surface People

Try to fully live our personal presences on the surface of the earth
Poetry becomes wings to fly and necessary fins to dive
All poetry is written for other places, connecting tomorrow with yesterday

7

Seven ravens are standing on this wasted shore
Here was a town until yesterday
Wasted, but also filled with light
And full of immaculateness that was never experienced before
The snowflakes on their black feathers are gradually melting
Becoming little drops of light
Temporarily abandoning the sky where the restless crows
And seagulls are racketing and circling
Seven ravens are watching over the shore
Because there are beings travelling right there
They are numberless, but neither a group nor a flock
One by one, one by one,
They cross the cold water,
Being washed by the beautiful light
Pouring down from between the dark clouds
The ravens are silently watching their departure

8

Father, the moon, I muttered
The moon had a size and brightness that I had never seen before
You once told me, "The moon is the soul of the sun"
Its light had no temperature
And its color was as white as the white of a black dog's eye
Under the moonlight we danced
Me and Mieko and Sakura danced with all our might like shadows
"In a certain American Indian tribe
When holding some kind of religious ritual
It doesn't begin
Until all who gathered laugh heartily"
Father, in barefoot
We took each other's hands and laughed, and we danced
It seemed that the moon also had a good laugh
Supermoon, the dirty photographs that the waves left behind
Start shining all at once

(*Translated from Japanese by the author*)

14

Hexaemeron

The Six Faces of Haphazard

ANDRÉ VALLIAS

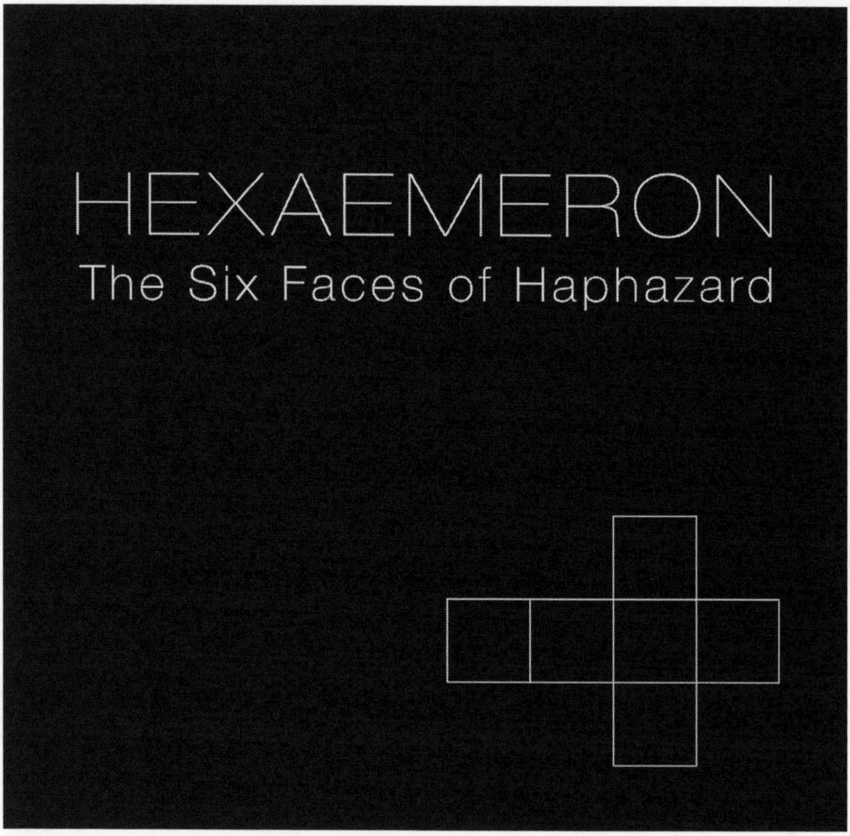
HEXAEMERON
The Six Faces of Haphazard

"Why did he make the whole creation not in one, or two, or three, or four, or five, but in six days? Such an one will learn this to be the truth of the matter — that, inasmuch as the angels are rational and mutable, one day would not have sufficed for their instruction if the whole had been produced in one day, for they would certainly have thought that things had been confusedly brought into existence like so many phantasms and been produced in disorder. But God Almighty having set apart one day for each single work, in due order formed the universe in parts, that it might be discriminated and thus better understood by the angels." **Cosmas Indicopleustes** (6th century)

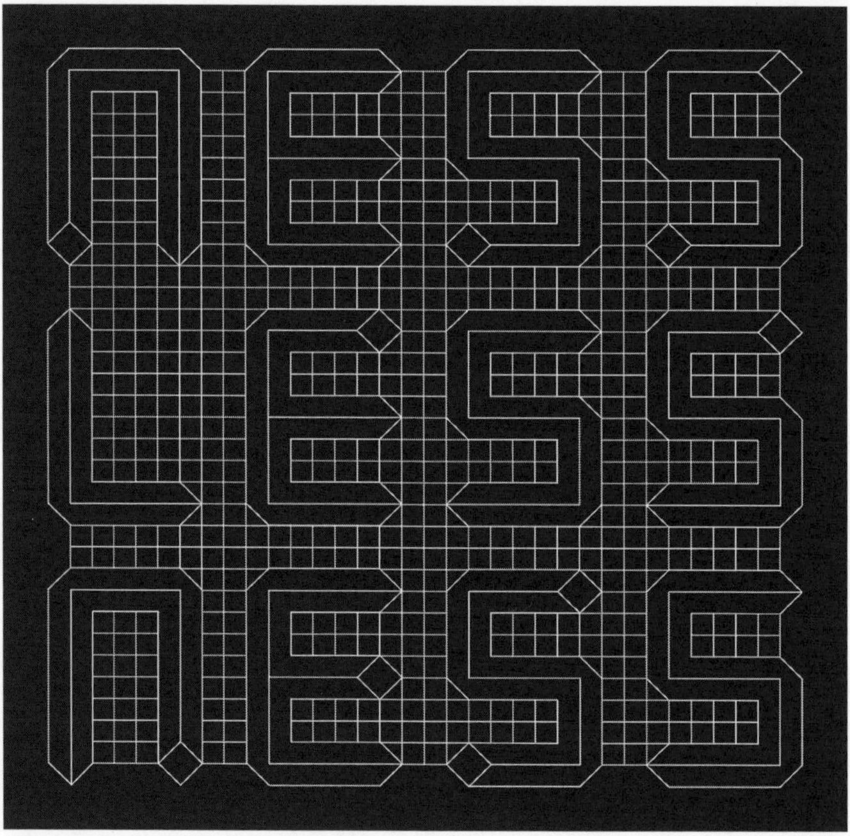
ness
less
ness

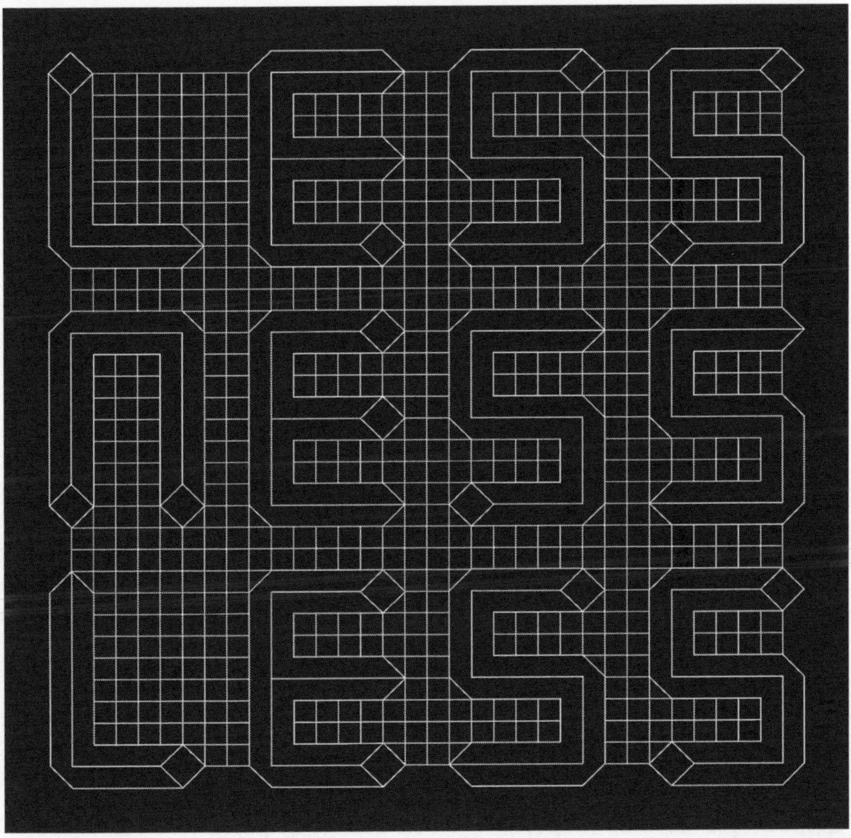

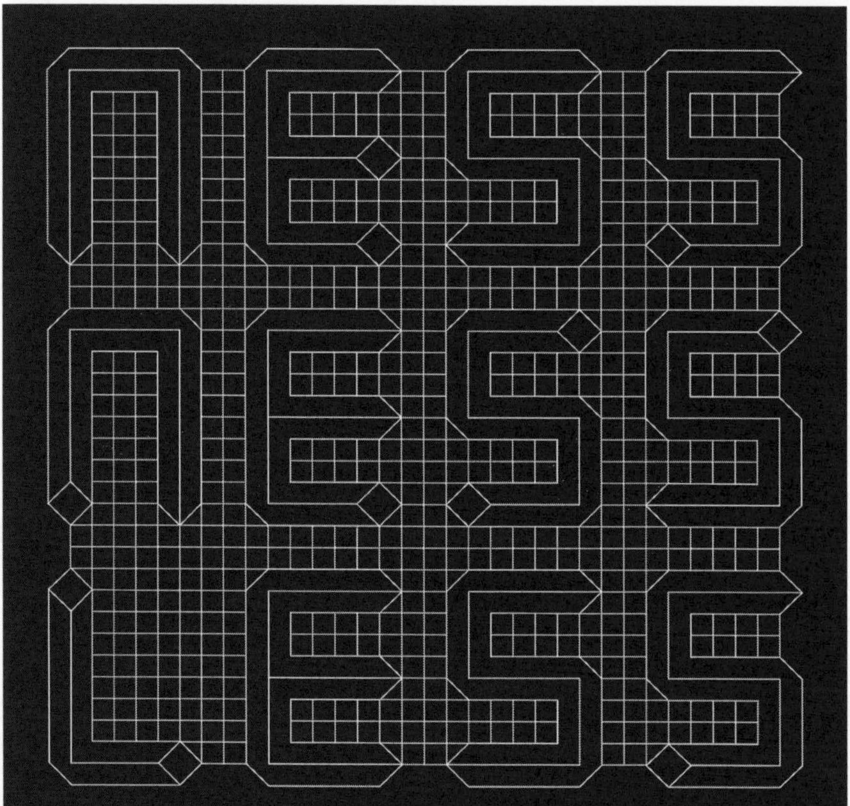
NESS
NESS
LESS

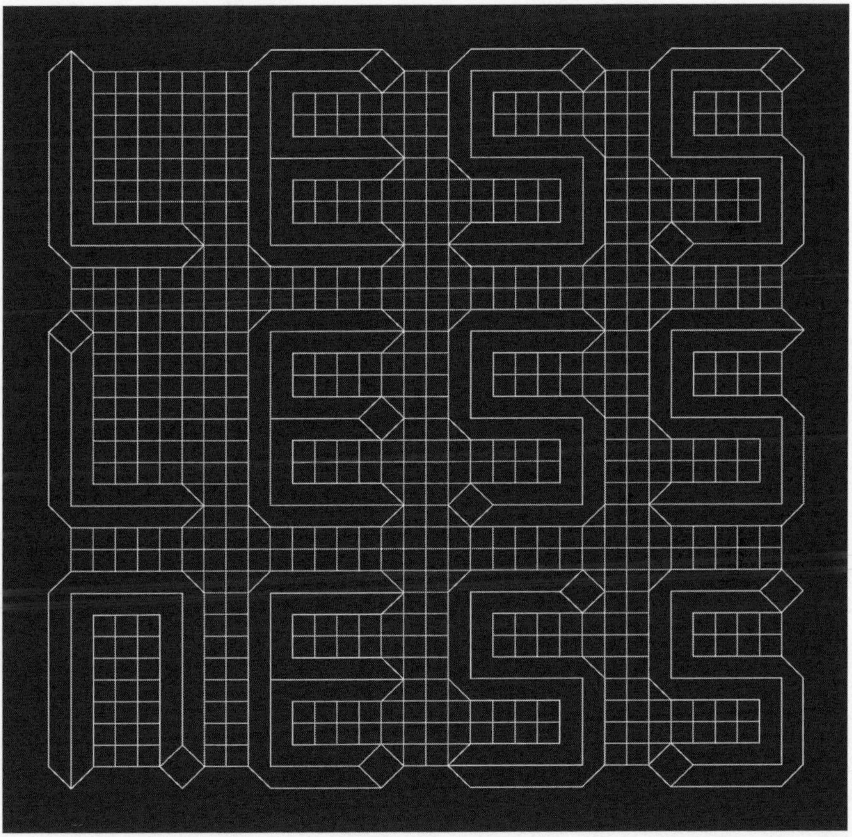
LESS
LESS
NESS

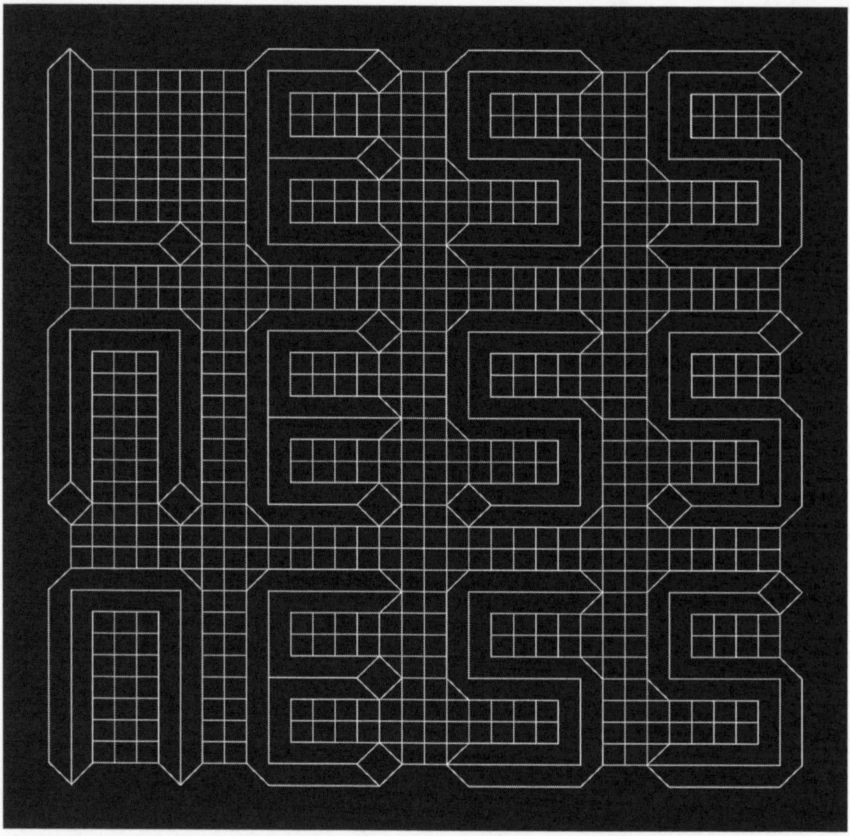
LESS
NESS
NESS

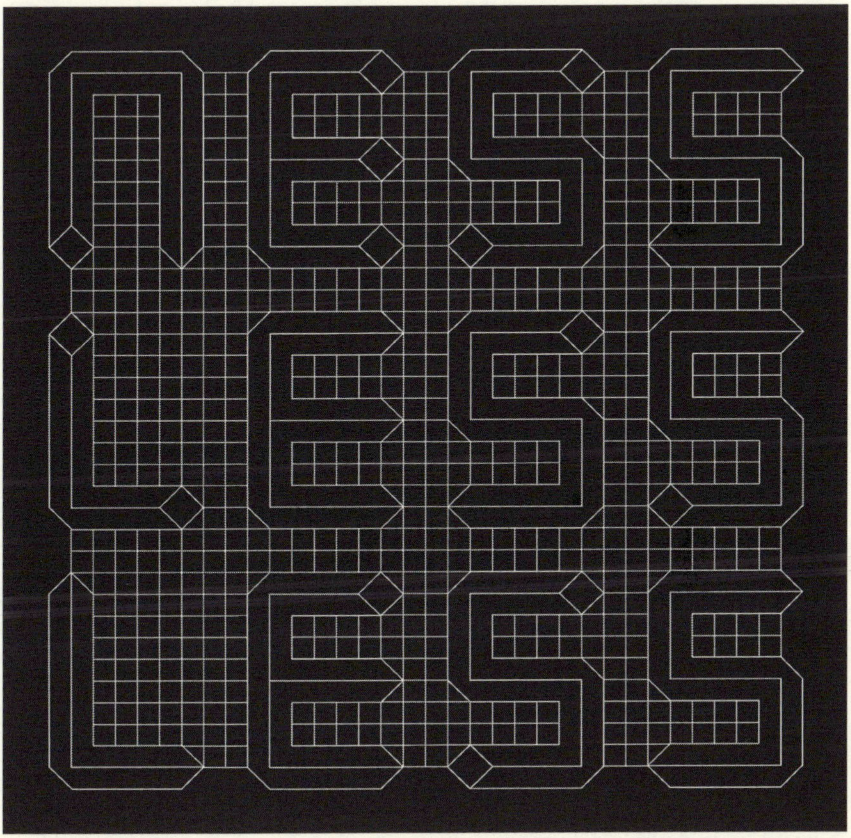

15

Amberianum (Philosophical Fragments of Caudio Amberian)

CHARLES BERNSTEIN

Abolens sensus numquam liberare cogitatione.
Abolishing reason will never free thought.

•

Etiam homo fastus scribere posse bonum carmen. Sed suus non amo.
Even a self-righteous man can write a good poem. But it's not likely.

•

Praecaveo osor qui clamat "odisti!"
Beware the bigot who shouts out "bigot!"

•

Nonnumquam homo qui mendacii loquimini veritatem.
Even a liar sometimes must tell the truth.

•

O dii magna! Protecut nobis adversum malis qui consumuntur per justitia.
May the gods save us from those consumed by their righteousness.

•

Colaphus est chiridotus punctum.
A cuff is not a sleeve.
(*Alt.:* A blow is not the full chemise.)

•

Aestas alga mutates in hiberna malogranatum
Summer seaweed becomes winter pomegranates.

•

Si paratextus fortior poema sequitur fornicando fortior amor?
If paratext is more important than poem, does it follow that love is more important than sex?

•

Perceptio est scriptum.
Perception is textual.

•

Omni scriptura est pupilla.
All texts are orphans.

•

Perspicientia est sensus vigalantis.
Knowledge is a matter of minding sense.

•

Ubi erraverit caper detondetur vitulum.
Where the goat strays the calf is shorn.

•

Rarus est maeror nomas.
Seldom is grief misplaced.

•

Omne iter fluxum.
Every journey takes a turn.

•

Cultura est opinabilis.
Cultivation is a manner of opinion.

•

In fragmenta veritas.
Truth is in pieces.

•

Vivis et vigeo. Argumentum injustitia deos.
The fact that you are alive and thriving is proof that the gods are not just.

•

Remissio prope nihil. Desiderium dono divum.
Forgiveness is overrated. Regret is a gift of gods.

•

Quid nunc videtur priori numquam imaginabilis.
What was unimaginable an hour ago is unforgettable now.

•

Proximi sui ruina unius hominis felicitatem.
One man's catastrophe is his neighbor's good fortune.

•

Servus absolvo illusion licentia. Dominus amat fraudis.
A slave is free of the illusion of freedom from which his master takes pleasure.

•

Virtus est selectivam.
Virtue is selective.

•

Coitus est bonitas plus quam amor. Est tangibili.
Sex is more virtuous than love because it is more tangible.

•

Amor abducit lubido.
Love turns many from desire.

•

In vino exiguum clinamen veritas.
In wine truth swerves.

•

Sensus mentis dolum.
Perception is the finest trick of the mind.

•

Veritas nondum visibilis.
The truth remains to be seen.

•

Salus in numeris donec numerus vester ascendit.
There is safety in numbers until your number is up.

•

Numquam nominare inane vacuum.
Never call a void a void.

•

Sine pullos nihilum ova.
If there were no chickens there'd be no eggs.

•

Ignorantiam didicit.
Ignorance is learned.

•

Odium contagiosa est.
Hatred is contagious.

•

Maximo sinceritatis ironia.
Irony is the perfection of sincerity.

•

Veritas est scortum sumptuosus
Truth is a pricey whore.

•

Judaeorum dabo optimus pretium.
Jews will give you the best price.

•

Si videris Judaeus, dicere salve pro me.
If you see a Jew be sure to say I said hello.

•

Omni infringes punctum impotens etiam amare.
Everything breaks at its weakest point including love.

•

Fragilitas solicito amatio.
Fragility is the root of love.

•

Quasi pardus est Judaeus. Sed absque maculis.
A Jew is like a leopard without the spots.[1]

Caudio Amberian was a Jewish poet and sophist of the first century A.D. (circa 30–75). He was likely born near Alexandria and spoke or read Aramaic, Hebrew, and Greek. He may have studied with Philo before moving to Rome around 60. In Rome, Amberian started a small school for sophistry, where he engaged students in Socratic-style dialogs. In addition, Amberian was a counselor to Nero in the last years of his reign, following the fire, and he helped set the ground for the move of Josephus and his entourage from Jerusalem to Rome in 71. The only previous translation of Amberian's work, an untitled poem, was published in Bernstein's *Girly Man*.

At school in Rome, Amebrian spoke in a broken or pidgin Latin that some of his students called "barbaric." The only record we have of his writing is the Latin transcriptions made by these notoriously unreliable and sometimes hostile students. The *Amberianum* was reconstructed from shreds and shards at the Sid Caesar Center for Dysraphic Studies. Missing words and the seaming of disconnected parts likely mar the work. The Latin manuscript was discovered on October 4, 1895, buried under a former Minsk dry goods store. The story of the miraculous finding of the *Amberianum* has been told in the award-winning book *The Oy! How the World Became Pataquerical.*

Acknowledgments

This book was born from Trans-Poetic Exchange: Around Blanco and "Campos de Paz," a two-day multimedia poetry show and colloquium that took place at Stanford University on January 29–30, 2010. Trans-Poetic Exchange was organized by the Department of Iberian and Latin American Cultures and co-sponsored by the Stanford Institute for Creativity and the Arts, and it brought together internationally renowned poets and scholars from Brazil, Catalonia, Japan, and the United States to share their perspectives on the poetic and intellectual worlds of Octavio Paz (1914–1998) and Haroldo de Campos (1929–2003). Many, but not all, of the contributors to this book were also participants at the conference.

We wish to take this opportunity to thank Joan Ramon Resina for having co-organized the colloquium with Marília Librandi, and Roland Greene and Robert Pogue Harrison for their participation in the event. We are especially indebted to the Catalan artist Frederic Amat for his contributions, including the creation of the cover art for this book. We are grateful to Augusto de Campos for supporting the event.

We would like to thank the graduate coordinators Mark Bajus and Hsiao-Shih (Raechel) Lee for the effort they devoted to the event, without which Trans-Poetic Exchange would never have been possible at the level in which it was organized. Their enthusiasm and commitment were greatly appreciated. Many thanks to Helga Wild for her assistance in the first stages of this manuscript, and to Vincent Barletta for revising its final version.

We are also grateful to Augusto de Campos, Inês Oseki-Dépré, Ivan Pérsio de Arruda Campos, Odile Cisneros, Maria Sylvia Nunes, Andrea Sanjad, and Nelson Sanjad for their support to this edited collection.

Notes

Introduction

1 See the introduction to Haroldo de Campos, *Galáxias* (São Paulo: Editora 34, 2004).

2 Alfred Gell, *Art and Agency: An Anthropological Theory* (Oxford: Clarendon, 1998), 98.

3 Gell, 98.

4 Octavio Paz, *The Collected Poems of Octavio Paz, 1957–1987*, ed. Eliot Weinberger (New York: New Directions, 1991), 311.

5 Kirsten Silva Gruesz, *Ambassadors of Culture: The Transamerican Origins of Latino Writing* (Princeton, NJ: Princeton University Press, 2001).

6 Octavio Paz, *La otra voz: Poesía y fin de siglo* (Barcelona: Seix Barral, 1990). For the concept of the "post-utopian poem," see Haroldo de Campos's influential essay "Poesia e modernidade: Da morte da arte à constelação. O poema pós-utópico," in *O arco-íris branco* (Rio de Janeiro: Imago, 1997), 243–269.

7 Ignacio Infante, *After Translation: The Transfer and Circulation of Modern Poetics across the Atlantic* (New York: Fordham University Press, 2013), 1.

8 Roberto Cantú, ed., *The Willow and the Spiral: Essays on Octavio Paz and the Poetic Imagination* (Newcastle: Cambridge Scholars Publishing, 2014).

9 See Lisa Block de Behar, ed., *Haroldo de Campos, don de poesía: Ensayos críticos sobre su obra* (Montevideo: Linardi y Risso, 2009); and Leda Tenório da Motta, ed., *Céu acima: Para um "tombeau" de Haroldo de Campos* (São Paulo: Perspectiva, 2005).

10 See Victoria Carpenter, "From Yellow to Red to Black: Tantric Reading of 'Blanco' by Octavio Paz," *Bulletin of Latin American Research* 21, no. 4 (2002): 527–544; Juan Malpartida, "Octavio Paz el traductor (Analogía y crítica)," *Revista de Occidente* 403 (2014): 36–61; and Clara Román-Odio, "'Blanco', a Western Mandala," *Revista Canadiense de Estudios Hispánicos* 24, no. 3 (2000): 503–515.

11 See, for example, Rodolfo Mata Sandoval, "Transblanco de Octavio Paz y Haroldo de Campos," *Vuelta* 216 (1994): 2; and "Haroldo de Campos y Octavio Paz: Del diálogo creativo a la mediación institucional en América Latina," *Latinoamérica*

30 (2001): 131–154. Additionally, see María Esther Maciel, "América Latina reinventada: Octavio Paz e Haroldo de Campos," *Revista Iberoamericana* 64, nos. 182–183 (1998): 219–228.

Chapter 1 On the Presence of Absence

1 See Enrico Mario Santí, "Esto no es un poema," in *Blanco/Archivo Blanco*, ed. Enrico Mario Santí (Mexico City: Ediciones del Equilibrista, 1995), 235–321; also in my *El acto de las palabras: Estudios y diálogos con Octavio Paz* (Mexico City: Fondo de Cultura Económica, 1997), 301–367 (333–399 in revised edition [2015]).
2 Octavio Paz, *Claude Lévi-Strauss: An Introduction*, trans. J. S. Bernstein (Ithaca, NY: Cornell University Press, 1970), 142.
3 Octavio Paz, *Alternating Current* (New York: Viking Press, 1973), 69.
4 *Claude Lévi-Strauss*, 142.
5 Santí, "Esto no es un poema," 310; and based on Octavio Paz communication from the Santí archive.
6 See Octavio Paz, *Ladera este (1962–1968)* (Mexico City: Joaquín Mortiz, 1969), 145–182; translation in *The Poems of Octavio Paz*, ed. and trans. Eliot Weinberger (New York: New Directions, 2014), 329–352.
7 *Blanco/Archivo Blanco*, 95.
8 *Blanco/Archivo Blanco*, 95 (emphasis is Paz's).
9 *The Poems of Octavio Paz*, 595 (in reference to 327).
10 See John M. Fein, *Toward Octavio Paz: A Reading of His Major Poems 1957–1976* (Lexington: University Press of Kentucky, 1986), 64–94.
11 See Eliot Weinberger, "Paz in Asia," in *Outside Stories* (New York: New Directions, 1992), 17–45; and Manuel Ulacia, *El árbol milenario: Un recorrido por la obra de Octavio Paz* (Barcelona: Galaxia Gutenberg, 1999), 225.
12 On "the middle way," see Shashibhusan Dasgupta, *An Introduction to Tantric Buddhism* (Calcutta: University of Calcutta, 1958).
13 See Pere Gimferrer, *Lecturas de Octavio Paz* (Barcelona: Anagrama, 1980), 59–71.
14 *Blanco/Archivo Blanco*, 310.
15 *The Poems of Octavio Paz*, 595.
16 *Blanco/Archivo Blanco*, 96.
17 All quotations from Paz letters are from *Blanco/Archivo Blanco*.
18 My thanks to my friend Vicente Molina Foix for allowing me access to this letter, dated July 19, 1991, from Octavio Paz.
19 On Amat's 2007 staging of the poem, see "Frederic Amat le da forma y escena al poema «Blanco», de Octavio Paz," ABC Cataluña, http://www.abc.es/hemeroteca/historico-04-12-2007/abc/Catalunya/frederic-amat-le-da-forma-y-escena-al-poema-blanco-de-octavio-paz_1641449475215.html (December 4, 2007, last accessed April 2019). My thanks to my friend Frederic Amat for sharing with me his DVD on *Blanco*. Additionally, Amat's image appears on the cover of this volume.

Chapter 2 "Blanco" and *Transblanco*

1 Namkhai Norbu, *Dzogchen: The Self-Perfected State*, trans. John Shane (New York: Snow Lion, 1989), 48.
2 Stéphane Mallarmé, "Ses purs ongles très haut dédiant leur onyx," in *Collected Poems*, trans. and with a commentary by Henry Weinfield, bilingual ed. (Berkeley: University of California Press, 1994), 69.

3 Ronaldo Brito, *Neoconcretismo. Vértice e ruptura do projeto construtivo brasileiro* (Rio de Janeiro: Funarte, 1985).

4 Emanuele Tesauro, "Arguzie umane," in *Il Cannocchiale Aristotelico o sia Idea dell'arguta et ingeniosa elocutione che serve à tutta l'arte oratoria, lapidaria; et simbolica esaminata co' principii del divino Aristotele*, 5th ed. (Turin: Bartolomeo Zavatta, 1670), 112.

Chapter 3 Refiguring the Poundian Ideogram

I am deeply indebted to José María Rodríguez García, without whose help with Spanish and Portuguese materials I could not have written this essay.

1 Octavio Paz to Haroldo de Campos, March 14, 1968, in Octavio Paz and Haroldo de Campos, *Transblanco (em torno a* Blanco *de Octavio Paz)* (São Paulo: Editora Siciliano, 1986), 100–101. I thank Antonio Sergio Bessa for his translation of this letter from Portuguese.

2 The translations are taken from Octavio Paz, *The Bow and the Lyre: The Poem. The Poetic Revelation. Poetry and History*, trans. Ruth L. C. Simms (Austin: University of Texas Press, 1973), 67–68. The first Spanish edition of *El arco y la lira (El poema. La revelación poética. Poesía e historia)* (1956) does not include Paz's patronizing comment on Pound's lack of a domestic tradition. This gloss, which supports the view that peripheral moderns have always sought the validation bestowed on their work by highbrow readers and critics in Paris and London, was tellingly first inserted in the French edition (*L'Arc et la lyre*, trans. Roger Munier [Paris: Gallimard, 1965]) and subsequently incorporated into later Spanish editions. See Paz, *El arco y la lira*, 2nd ed., rev. (Mexico City: Fondo de Cultura Económica, 1967), 80: "Pound nos propone una tradición: Confucio, Malatesta, Adams, Odiseo . . . La verdad es que nos propone tantas y tan diversas porque él mismo no tiene ninguna."

3 Paz's "¿Poesía latinoamericana?" was written in Delhi in 1967 and first published in English as "The Word as Foundation," *Times Literary Supplement*, November 14, 1968, 1283–1284. The Spanish version was included in the poet's 1973 miscellaneous essay collection, *El signo y el garabato* (Barcelona: Seix Barral, 1991), 187; my translation is from the Spanish original. This dismissal of Pound as conquistador echoes Paz's larger mistrust of the Western translator's penchant to cannibalize non-Western materials. See José María Rodríguez García's "Literary into Cultural Translation," in "Literature into Cultural Translation," ed. J. M. Rodríguez García, special issue, *diacritics* 34, nos. 3–4 (Fall-Winter 2004): 13–16, esp. 13n6. Paz insistently connects U.S. imperialism to the nation's conflicted Puritan origins very much in the same way as he attributes to Pound the need to overcompensate for American literature's Emersonian lack of cultural contacts with the Old World: "The Puritan tradition, in stressing separation, becomes antihistorical and isolationist" (Esa tradición puritana, al acentuar la separación, es ahistórica y aislacionista). Consequently, "when the United States abandon their isolation to take part in the affairs of this world, they behave like a believer in the land of the infidels" (Cuando los Estados Unidos abandonan su aislamiento y participan en los negocios de este mundo lo hacen como el creyente en tierra de infieles). See Paz, *Tiempo nublado* (Barcelona: Seix Barral, 1983), 56.

4 Stéphane Mallarmé, *Collected Poems*, trans. and with a commentary by Henry Weinfield, bilingual ed. (Berkeley: University of California Press, 1994), 121

(emphasis mine). References to the text of this translation will subsequently be given as "Weinfield" followed by the appropriate page numbers. For the poem itself, see Weinfield, 124–145. For a facsimile copy of the printing in *Cosmopolis*, the original French text of the headnote, and an updated critical edition of the poem, see Mallarmé, *Œuvres complètes*, ed. Bertrand Marchal (Paris: Gallimard, 1998), 363–407.

5 Weinfield, 121–122.

6 Weinfield, 138–139.

7 Ezra Pound, "Canto 77," in *The Cantos* (New York: New Directions, 1970), 466.

8 Octavio Paz, "Blanco," in *The Collected Poems of Octavio Paz: 1957–1987*, trans. and ed. Eliot Weinberger (New York: New Directions, 1991), 311. This bilingual edition will subsequently be cited as "Weinberger," although it also features some illustrious secondary translators whose names will be given as needed. An earlier translation of "Blanco," signed by G. Aroul and Charles Tomlinson (a longtime collaborator of Paz's), was included in the following bilingual anthology: Octavio Paz, *Configurations*, with an introduction by Muriel Rukeyser (New York: New Directions, 1971), 175–195.

9 Weinberger, 311.

10 Weinberger, 314–316.

11 Weinberger, 315–317.

12 There is one exception in the next section, where David Livingstone's words about his adventures in South Africa—"Patience, patience" and "river rising a little"—are introduced in English (Weinberger, 316–317). In the late surrealist poem "Salamandra" (included in the 1962 collection *Salamandra (1958–1961)* and in Weinberger, 138–149; trans. Denise Levertov), the amphibian animal of that name is represented as enduring and surviving fire: "El fuego es su pasión es su *paciencia*" (Weinberger, 148; italics in the original), which emphatically plays on our sequential reading of both "Paz" and "ciencia" in the *space* of one word. The implication for readers of Rimbaud (one of Paz's intellectual and moral icons) is that Rimbaud's *alchimie du verbe* and Paz's "science of patience" are emblematized through the multiple associations triggered by the quiet and resilient yet also fiery salamander. Like "Blanco," the poem "Salamandra" also cites verbatim pre-existing literary and cultural texts without explicitly acknowledging the source.

13 The book that collects this translation is Octavio Paz and Haroldo de Campos's *Transblanco*. Besides including the full text of Paz's *Blanco* in Spanish alongside Haroldo's Portuguese version (no page numbers are used), it features brief early assessments of their literary relation, such as their mutual indebtedness to the Mallarméan and Poundian traditions. See Emir Rodríguez Monegal, "Blanco/ Branco: Transblanco," in Octavio Paz and Haroldo de Campos, *Transblanco: em torno a Blanco de Octavio Paz* (São Paulo: Siciliano, 1994), 13–19.

14 Haroldo de Campos, *Galáxias* (São Paulo: Editora Ex Libris, 1984).

15 Haroldo de Campos, "The Open Work of Art" [1955], trans. Jon Tolman, in *Novas: Selected Writings*, ed. Antonio Sergio Bessa and Odile Cisneros (Evanston, IL: Northwestern University Press, 2007), 220. Unless otherwise indicated, translations of all essays cited from this anthology are by one of the two editors.

16 Campos, 221.

17 Campos, 222.

18 Haroldo de Campos, "The Informational Temperature of the Text" [1960], trans. Jon Tolman, in Campos, *Novas*, 230.

19 Campos, 232, 234 (emphasis mine).

20 Haroldo de Campos, "Anthropophagous Reason: Dialogue and Difference in Brazilian Culture" [1981], in Campos, *Novas*, 176, 177.

21 Haroldo de Campos, "Poetic Function and Ideogram / The Sinological Argument" [1981], trans. Kevin Mundy and Marc Benson, in Campos, *Novas*, 287–311. I discuss Haroldo's argument in "From Avant-Garde to Digital: The Legacy of Brazilian Concrete Poetry," in *Unoriginal Genius: Poetry by Other Means in the New Century* (Chicago: University of Chicago Press, 2010), 50–75.

22 Haroldo de Campos, "The Ghost in the Text (Saussure and the Anagrams)" [1976], trans. Craig D. Dworkin, in Campos, *Novas*, 282.

23 Campos, "Anthropophagous Reason," 170.

24 Haroldo de Campos, "Author's Note," *Galáxias*, trans. Odile Cisneros, http://www.artsrn.ualberta.ca/galaxias/acknowledgements.html.

25 Weinberger, 330–331.

26 Odile Cisneros and Suzanne Jill Levine have a translation of the *Galáxias* into English, and there are translations by Sergio Bessa and Charles A. Perrone in Campos, *Novas*, 121–131. But sonically, the French translation is much closer to the Portuguese than any English one could be, so I use the French here.

27 Charles Baudelaire, "Le Voyage," in *Œuvres complètes*, ed. Claude Pichois (Paris: Gallimard, 1961), 122. In English: "For the child, in love with maps and stamps / The universe is equal to his vast appetite. / Ah, how large the world is in the evening lamplight! / To the eye of memory, how the world is small!"

28 Haroldo de Campos, *Galaxies*, with a preface by Jacques Roubaud, trans. and introduction by Inês Oseki-Dépré and the author (Paris: La Main Courante, 1998). Like the Portuguese-language original, the French translation does not use page numbers. Both editions arrange the series of page-long texts in chronological order, beginning with the earliest date of composition. An index lists the initial words of each galaxy followed by its date of composition in parentheses.

29 Weinberger, 330–331.

30 These are the book citations in all three languages: Octavio Paz, *Le singe grammairien*, trans. Claude Esteban (Geneva: A. Skira, 1972); *El mono gramático* (Barcelona: Seix Barral, 1974); *The Monkey Grammarian*, trans. Helen R. Lane (New York: Seaver Books-Grove Press, 1981).

31 See José María Rodríguez García, "John Donne after Octavio Paz: Translation as Transculturation," *Dispositio/n: American Journal of Cultural Histories and Theories* 48 (1999): 166–172; see also email note to the author, March 10, 2010. Rodríguez García praises Paz's learning, ingeniousness, and surrealist wordplay in *The Monkey Grammarian* and in the translation of John Donne's "Elegy 19: To His Mistress Going to Bed," but he is quite critical of Paz's recourse to pornography and his phallocentric vision; see esp. "John Donne after Octavio Paz," 166–167. See also Jason Wilson, *Octavio Paz: A Study of His Poetics* (Cambridge: Cambridge University Press, 1979), 149–165.

32 Weinberger, 328–329.

Chapter 4 Poetry Makes Nothing Happen

1 Octavio Paz and Haroldo de Campos, *Transblanco* (São Paulo: Siciliano, 1986).

2 Haroldo de Campos, "Author's Note," *Galáxias*, trans. Odile Cisneros and Suzanne Jill Levine, http://www.artsrn.ualberta.ca/galaxias/index.html (last

accessed October 2019). Unless otherwise indicated, all translations of passages from *Galáxias* are from these translators.

3 Stéphane Mallarmé, *Collected Poems*, trans. and with a commentary by Henry Weinfield, bilingual ed. (Berkeley: University of California Press, 1994), 121.

4 Mallarmé, sonnet "Ses purs ongles très haut dédiant leur onyx," often called the "Ptyx Sonnet" or the "Sonnet en -ix," in *Collected Poems*, 69.

5 Mallarmé, "Preface," in *Collected Poems*, 122.

6 Jean Baudrillard, "The Art of Disappearance," in *Jean Baudrillard: Art and Artefact*, ed. Nicholas Zurbrugg (London: Sage Publications, 1997), 28–31.

7 Mallarmé, "Preface," in *Collected Poems*, 122.

8 Fernando Pessoa, "Opiário," in *Ficções do interlúdio*, ed. Fernando Cabral Martins (Lisbon: Assírio & Alvim, 1998), 105.

9 From W. H. Auden, *Another Time* (New York: Random House, 1940). Published by Random House. Copyright © 1940 W. H. Auden, renewed by the Estate of W. H. Auden. Used by permission of Curtis Brown, Ltd.

10 Joseph Brodsky, "On 'September 1, 1939' by W. H. Auden," in *Less Than One: Selected Essays* (New York: Farrar, Straus and Giroux, 1988), 361.

11 Brodsky, 364.

12 Haroldo de Campos, *Galáxias*, 2nd ed., rev. (São Paulo: Editora 34, 2004).

13 While the Nasrid kingdom of Granada fell to the Catholic monarchs in 1492, its Muslim inhabitants were not forced to convert to Christianity until 1502 and did not suffer mass expulsion (converts or not) until 1571, at the end of the Second Alpujarras War.

14 Antonio Machado, *Poesias de Guerra (1936–1939). Border of a Dream. Selected Poems*, bilingual ed., trans. and introduction by Willis Barnstone (Port Townsend, WA: Copper Canyon Press, 2004).

15 In Octavio Paz, *The Collected Poems of Octavio Paz: 1957–1987*, trans. and ed. Eliot Weinberger (New York: New Directions, 1991), 225–226.

16 Manuel da Nóbrega, "Carta (1549)," in *Cartas dos primeiros jesuitas no Brasil*, vol. 1, ed. Serafim Leite (Lisbon: Livraria Portugalia, 1956), 142.

17 Davi Kopenawa and Bruce Albert, *A queda do céu: Palavras de um xamã yanomami*, trans. Beatriz Perrone-Moisés (São Paulo: Companhia das Letras, 2010).

Chapter 5 Haroldo de Campos, Octavio Paz, and the Experience of the Avant-Garde

1 Haroldo de Campos, "Poesia e modernidade: Da morte da arte à constelação. O poema pós-utópico," in *O arco-íris branco* (Rio de Janeiro: Imago, 1997), 243–269.

2 Octavio Paz, "Poetry and Modernity," trans. Eliot Weinberger, in *The Tanner Lectures on Human Values*, delivered at the University of Utah, October 18–20, 1989, http://tannerlectures.utah.edu/_documents/a-to-z/p/Paz98.pdf.

3 Campos, "Poesia e modernidade," 268–269.

4 Paz, "Poetry and Modernity," 75.

5 Campos, "Poesia e modernidade," 268.

6 Ernst Bloch, *Das Prinzip Hoffnung* (Frankfurt an Main: Suhrkamp, 1959).

7 Campos, "Poesia e modernidade," 268.

8 My reflections on this subject have been developed in Cicero, *O mundo desde o fim* (São Paulo: Companhia das Letras, 2005).

9 Cicero, 256.
10 Paz, "Poetry and Modernity," 59.
11 Immanuel Kant, *Kritik der reinen Vernunft* (Frankfurt am Main: Suhrkamp, 1976), xii, note.
12 Paz, "Poetry and Modernity," 58.
13 Stéphane Mallarmé, "Observation relative au poème 'Un coup de dés jamais n'abolira le Hasard,'" in *Oeuvres complètes*, ed. Bertrand Marchal (Paris: Gallimard, 1998), 392.
14 Ezra Pound, *ABC of Reading* (New York: New Directions, 1934), 28, 14.
15 Arthur Rimbaud, "Mouvement," in *L'oeuvre* (Paris: Textuel, 2000), 409.

Chapter 6 "Blanco"

This essay is for Augusto de Campos, with the concrete gusto of friendship. It was translated by Sueli Cavendish.

1 Augusto de Campos and Haroldo de Campos published *Sousândrade: O terremoto clandestino* (Rio de Janeiro: Instituto Nacional do Livro) in 1964.
2 Eduardo Milán, "Tensão do dizer em *Blanco* de Octavio Paz," in *Transblanco*, ed. Octavio Paz and Haroldo de Campos (São Paulo: Agência Siciliano, 1986), 167.
3 The translation into English follows the version from *The Collected Poems of Octavio Paz (1957–1987)*, ed. and trans. Eliot Weinberger, with additional translations by Elizabeth Bishop, Paul Blackburn, et al. (New York: New Directions, 1991).
4 Milán, "Tensão do dizer em *Blanco* de Octavio Paz," 168.
5 Milán, 169.
6 Blocks or pages? I prefer the formulation because in the Brazilian edition of *Transblanco* the segments that I have highlighted in both the Spanish text and its Portuguese transcreation appear on separate pages. Thus, for instance, the erotic aspect of the world—"los ríos de tu cuerpo"—stands face to face to "la tierra calcinada." In Weinberger's bilingual translation, there is larger spacing that shapes and contours blocks, making their pagination and progression somewhat different. It is for that reason that I like to think of "Blanco" in blocks.
7 Julio Ortega, "*Blanco:* Space of Change," *World Literature Today* 56, no. 4 (Autumn 1982): 637.
8 It is in this verse, 221, right stanza, where I have made the translation my own. In the Weinberger text it is translated as "thought phallus and word vulva" (instead of "word womb").
9 Milán, "Tensão do dizer em *Blanco* de Octavio Paz," 166.
10 Michel Foucault, *Les mots et les choses* (Paris: Gallimard, 1966), 32.
11 Foucault, 58.
12 Foucault, 51.
13 See Kerstin Behnke, "Krise der Repräsentation," item V from "Repräsentation," in *Historisches Wörterbuch der Philosophie*, ed. Joachim Ritter and Karlfried Gründer (Darmstadt: Wissenschaftliche Buchgesellschaft, 1992), 8:849.
14 Foucault, *Les Mots et les choses*, 58.
15 Foucault, 58.
16 Foucault, 63.
17 Foucault, 315.

18 Foucault, 317.
19 Foucault, 317.
20 Foucault, 317.
21 Foucault, 316–317.
22 Jacques Derrida, "La double séance" [1970], republished in *La dissémination* (Paris: Seuil, 1972), 240.
23 Wolfgang Iser, *Das Fiktive und das Imaginäre: Perspektiven literarischer Anthropologie* (Frankfurt am Main: Suhrkamp, 1991); translated as *The Fictive and the Imaginary: Charting Literary Anthropology* (Baltimore: Johns Hopkins University Press, 1993).

Chapter 7 Translation and Radical Poetics

This chapter was originally published in Spanish as "Traducción y poéticas radicales: El caso de Octavio Paz y el grupo *noigandres*," in *Estudios hispánicos en el siglo XXI*, a special volume edited by Ana Kuzmanović Jovanović, Jelena Filipović, Jasna Stojanović, and Jelena Rajić to commemorate the fortieth anniversary of the Spanish Language and Literature Department at the University of Belgrade. That version is available online at http://www.fil.bg.ac.rs/lang/sr/estudios-hispanicos-en-el-siglo-xxi/.

1 There are some studies on the relationship between Octavio Paz and Haroldo de Campos, which I briefly discuss below. The only one that, to my knowledge, specifically compares their translation theories is, interestingly, Campos's reflection on *Transblanco*, his translation or "transcreation" of Paz's poem "Blanco." In that essay, Campos emphasizes the similarities between their theoretical reflections, suggesting that the disjunction between analogue translation (i.e., translating meaning) and translation as creation, which Paz proposed in "The Literal and the Literary," could be subsumed within a broader concept of "transcreation" (poderia ser subsumida num conceito mais amplo de transcriação). Campos, however, does not analyze Paz's translations. Octavio Paz and Haroldo de Campos, *Transblanco: Em torno a* Blanco *de Octavio Paz*, 2nd ed. (São Paulo: Editora Siciliano, 1994), 189.
2 Of the various authors who compared the work of Paz and Campos, I would like to briefly highlight three. Maria Esther Maciel argues that both try to "place Latin America on the global circuit of creative exchanges," contributing to "the opening of Latin American culture to the influence of other cultures [. . . in] an equally pluralized and de-centered universality" (my translation from Portuguese). "América Latina Reinventada: Octavio Paz e Haroldo De Campos," *Revista Iberoamericana* 64, nos. 182–183 (1998): 219. Manuel Ulacia compares the impact of Haroldo de Campos on Octavio Paz's work in "El Árbol Milenario: Octavio Paz y Haroldo De Campos," *Siglo XX/20th Century* 10, nos.1–2 (1992): 221. Tania Franco Carvalhal notes that both writers, "despite belonging to different literary contexts, discovered, around the same time, identical sources of inspiration and dealt with the same literary issues" (my translation from French). "La tradition du Haikú dans la poésie latine-américaine: Un cas de médiation," in *ICLA '91 Tokyo: The Force of Vision, II: Visions in History; Visions of the Other*, ed. Earl Miner et al. (Tokyo: Internat. Compar. Lit. Assn., 1995), 384. None of these authors, however, comparatively examine their ideas on translation or their translations.

3 In a conversation with Campos, Lafer describes his relationship with Paz. "Conversación sobre Octavio Paz," *Cuadernos Hispanoamericanos: Revista Mensual de Cultura Hispánica* 558 (1996): 7–27.

4 It is not often acknowledged that Campos's was the first translation of Paz's poetry into Portuguese.

5 Translations of texts in Portuguese and in Spanish, unless otherwise indicated, are mine. I use the English version in the general text and the original in the notes. "Tradição metafórica e retórico-discursiva característica da poesia espanhola e hispano-americana deste século." Paz and Campos, *Transblanco*, 94.

6 "Aos poemas breves, despojados, que têm a ver com o haicai e a sintaxe da montagem; e também aos poemas sobre a mecânica do próprio poema—poemas metalingüísticos—, nos quais a poesia se faz do seu próprio fazer." Paz and Campos, 94.

7 Paz and Campos, 96–101.

8 Paz and Campos, 97.

9 "Muito poucas obras de poesia, nos últimos anos, me deram a alegria e as surpresas que encontrei nos poemas seus, de Augusto de Campos, de Décio Pignatari e de seus demais amigos." Paz's remarks appear in Portuguese because I am quoting from Campos's edition of their correspondence, which does not include Paz's letters in the original Spanish. Paz and Campos, 97.

10 "E algo muito amplo, um enfoque geral, uma atitude metódica, que pode envolver desde o poema de uma só palavra ou de signos visuais artificiais (os 'poemas-código' de Décio Pignatari) até composições muito complexas (como os poemas em cor de Augusto, a 'Estela cubana' de Pignatari, ou minha prosa em progresso)." Paz and Campos, 107–109.

11 In "From Isomorphism to Cannibalism: The Evolution of Haroldo de Campos's Translation Concepts," I argue that the concept of "transcriação" (transcreation) developed by Haroldo and practiced by the Noigandres group emerged precisely from the practice of concrete poetry with its isomorphic mirroring of form and content. *Traduction, Terminologie, Rédaction* 25, no. 2 (2012): 23–25.

12 "Admitida a tese da impossibilidade em princípio da tradução de textos criativos, parece-nos que esta engendra o corolário da possibilidade, também em princípio, da recriação desses textos. Teremos, como quer Bense, em outra língua, uma outra informação estética, autônoma, mas ambas estarão ligadas entre si por uma relação de isomorfia: serão diferentes enquanto linguagem, mas, como os corpos isomorfos, cristalizar-se-ão dentro de um mesmo sistema." Original Portuguese in Haroldo de Campos, "Da tradução como criação e crítica," in *Metalinguagem e outras metas: Ensaios de teoria e crítica literária* (São Paulo: Editora Perspectiva, 1992), 34; translation appears in Haroldo de Campos, Antonio Sergio Bessa, and Odile Cisneros, "Translation as Creation and Criticism," in *Novas: Selected Writings* (Evanston, IL: Northwestern University Press, 2007), 315.

13 First published in English in the *Times Literary Supplement*, September 18, 1970. Since no translator is acknowledged, the author of the English version of this essay is probably Paz himself, who lived in Cambridge at the time. The Spanish version, "Traducción: Literatura y literalidad," was later included in 1971 in a volume with the same title, along with other essays on translation, which were later incorporated into *El signo y el garabato* (1972).

14 "Los significados del poema son múltiples y cambiantes; las palabras del mismo poema son únicas e insustituibles. Cambiarlas sería destruir el poema." Octavio

Paz, "Traducción: Literatura y literalidad," in *Traducción: Literatura y literalidad* (Barcelona: Tusquets Editor, 1971), 15; translation in Octavio Paz, "The Literal and the Literary," *TLS: The Times Literary Supplement*, September 18, 1970, 1020.

15 "En otro lenguaje y con signos diferentes . . . componer un poema análogo al original." Paz, "Traducción," 16; translation, Paz, "The Literal and the Literary," 1021.

16 "[A] 'sentença absoluta,' . . . 'que não tem outro conteúdo senão sua estrutura.'" Campos, "Tradução," 31; translation in Campos, Bessa, and Cisneros, "Translation as Creation and Criticism," 312.

17 "Cada lectura es una traducción y cada crítica es, o comienza por ser, una interpretación." Paz, "Traducción," 16; translation, Campos, Bessa, and Cisneros, "Translation as Creation and Criticism," 312; Paz, "The Literal and the Literary," 1020–1021.

18 Campos wrote: "I drank the mescalina of myself, and I went from dusk till dawn / translating 'Blanco' by Octavio Paz" (Tomei a mescalina de mim mesmo, e passei esta noite em claro / traduzindo "Blanco" de Octavio Paz). Paz and Campos, *Transblanco*, 118.

19 In chemistry, isomorphism refers to "the existence of two or more substances (*isomorphs*) that have the same crystal structure." John Daintith, "Isomorphism," in *Dictionary of Chemistry*, 6th ed. (Oxford: Oxford University Press, 2008), DOI: 10.1093/acref/9780199204632.001.000.

20 "[A] tradução não é apenas criativa e crítica, mas também implica uma atividade combinatória que desencadeia funções não previstas ou talvez latentes na língua." Paz and Campos, *Transblanco*, 119, 145.

21 "Quanto ao ritmo, que é o mais difícil de traduzir, o grande obstáculo com que nos defrontamos nós todos, tradutores de poesia: até onde posso julgar, parece-me que você conseguiu reproduzir a polimetria do original. Também é notável—outra proeza—que você tenha encontrado as equivalências das aliterações, paronomásias e outros ecos verbais." Paz and Campos, *Transblanco*, 119.

22 Octavio Paz, *Excursiones/incursiones: Dominio extranjero*, 2nd ed. (Barcelona: Círculo de Lectores, 1994), 100.

23 Paz, 101.

24 Augusto de Campos et al., *Mallarmé* (São Paulo: Editora Perspectiva, 1974), 74.

25 "Dei especial atenção, nas traduções, aos jogos vocabulares da poesia de Mallarmé—paronomásias, assonâncias, aliterações—nos quais a rima tem papel de destaque. As rimas mallarmeanas—rimas equívocas, rimas homófonas, rimas leoninas, que se ecoam, se devoram e se entreespelham—contribuem decisivamente para romper, com suas associações verticais, o encadeamento linear do verso. Não hesitei em chegar a soluções extremadas, que, embora inexistentes por vezes num trecho particular do original, parecem-me justificar-se plenamente dentro da poética mallarmaica." Augusto de Campos, "Mallarmé," 28.

26 In Paz's defense, we can cite the exegetical essay "El *Soneto en ix* de Mallarmé," where Paz also justifies his translation choices. There he argues that it would have been impossible to keep the rhymes in *ix* in Spanish and recognizes that "although the closest and most immediate model of a translation of this kind would be *modernista* poetry . . . with regard to the syntax, I availed myself of the examples afforded by our baroque poets" (hubiera sido imposible conservar en español las rimas en *ix*; aunque el modelo más inmediato y afín de una traducción de esta índole sea la versificación modernista . . . por lo que toca a la sintaxis, me acogí al ejemplo de nuestros poetas barrocos). Paz, *Excursiones/incursiones*, 111.

27 "Uma das mais densas imagens de solidão que se conhecem, no que se poderia chamar de haicai da folha-que-cai." ee cummings and Augusto de Campos, *40 Poem(a)s*, 2nd ed. (São Paulo: Brasiliense, 1986), 25–26.
28 Octavio Paz and Nicanor Vélez, *Versiones y diversiones*, bilingual ed. (Barcelona: Galaxia Gutenberg, Círculo de Lectores, 2000), 308.
29 Paz and Vélez, 180–181.
30 Manuel Ulacia notes that "a classical equilibrium position in the work of Octavio Paz is related to his poetics of reconciliation of opposites" (my translation from Spanish). "El Árbol Milenario," 221.
31 cummings and Campos, *40 Poem(a)s*, 25–31.
32 cummings and Campos, 29.
33 See Paz, *Excursiones*, 305.
34 "Pocas veces los poetas son buenos traductores. No lo son porque casi siempre usan el poema ajeno como un punto de partida para escribir su poema." Paz, "Traducción," 14; translation in Paz, "The Literal and the Literary," 1020.
35 In 1993 Paz published the book-length essay *La llama doble: Amor y erotismo* (*The Double Flame: Love and Eroticism*).
36 Augusto de Campos, *Poesia da recusa* (São Paulo: Perspectiva, 2006), 17.
37 Haroldo de Campos, "Anthropophagous Reason: Dialogue and Difference in Brazilian Culture," in *Novas: Selected Writings* (Evanston, IL: Northwestern University Press, 2007), 173.

Chapter 8 Pages, Pageants, Portraits, Prospects

1 This chapter is an adapted translation of the text of an invited illustrated talk delivered July 24, 2013, at the Espaço Haroldo de Campos de Poesia e Literatura within the municipal arts venue Casa das Rosas in São Paulo. The contiguous Centro de Referência Haroldo de Campos features the poet-professor's extensive library of literature and criticism in multiple languages. A series of events in 2013 marked the tenth anniversary of the passing of the highly distinguished scholar and artist of the word. Naturally, as this was originally a talk and not an essay, it should be read with that tone—and one of remembrance—in mind.
2 Allusion to *Pauliceia Desvairada* (1922) by Mário de Andrade, a fundamental work of Brazilian modernist poetry, translated as *Hallucinated City* by Jack Tomlins without reference to the name São Paulo. The title of Haroldo's poetry book cites a memorable phrase of Karl Marx's in *Economic and Philosophic Manuscripts of 1844*.
3 The posting is available at http://translationjournal.net/journal/39prof.htm.
4 *Texas Quarterly* (Winter 1972): 112–160.
5 Haroldo de Campos, "Hölderlin's Red Word," trans. Albert Bork, *20th Century Studies*, no. 11, 1974: 4–10.
6 K. David Jackson and Albert Bork, trans., *Seraphim Grosse Pointe* (Austin: Nefertiti Head Press, 1979).
7 Haroldo de Campos, "A linguagem do Iauaretê" [1962], in *Metalinguagem: Ensaios de teoria e crítica literária* (São Paulo: Perspectiva, 1976).
8 Charles A. Perrone, "Notas para facilitar a leitura de 'Meu tio o iauaretê,'" *Hispania* 91, no. 4 (2008): 766–774.
9 Haroldo de Campos, *O sequestro do Barroco na formação da literatura brasileira: O caso Gregório de Matos* (São Paulo: Perspectiva, 1989).

10 December 4, 1995. See page 307 in Bernard McGuirk and Else R. P. Vieira, eds., *Haroldo de Campos: In Conversation* (London: Zoilus Press, 2009).

11 Charles A. Perrone, "De Gregório de Matos a Caetano Veloso e 'Outras palavras': Barroquismo na Música Popular Brasileira contemporânea," *Revista iberoamericana* 50, no. 126 (1984): 77–99. Reprinted in *Barroco* 13 (1985): 107–123; and in *Barroco: Teoria e análise*, ed. Affonso Ávila (São Paulo: Perspectiva, 1997), 333–347.

12 Haroldo de Campos, "Translatio," in *Transblanco*, ed. Octavio Paz and Haroldo de Campos (São Paulo: Agência Siciliano, 1986), 118.

13 Christopher Middleton and Norman Potter, trans., "passtimes & killtimes," *Via* 1 (May 1976): 55–57.

14 Ewing Campbell and Julio Ortega, eds., *The Plaza of Encounters* (Austin: Latitudes Press, 1981), 36–37.

15 Julio Ortega, "Concrete Poetry and Beyond: A Conversation between Julio Ortega and Haroldo de Campos," *Review: Literature and Arts of the Americas* 19, no. 36 (1986): 36–45.

16 Haroldo de Campos, *Novas: Selected Writings*, ed. Antonio Sergio Bessa and Odile Cisneros (Evanston, IL: Northwestern University Press, 2007).

17 Available at http://www.artsrn.ualberta.ca/galaxias/index.html.

18 Marco de Oliveira. See http://gringocarioca.com, and click the "recreations" button, then "Haroldo de Campos," "borndead."

19 Charles A. Perrone, "4×3×2=Quadrangulating Triangular Pairs: Simultaneous Versions of a Vital Concrete Poem," *Tradução em revista* 6 (2009): 1–17.

Chapter 9 "Logopéia via Goethe via Christopher Middleton"

I am grateful to the Casa das Rosas (São Paulo) for the invitation to present a tape recording of readings by Haroldo de Campos, if not lost then at least misplaced for more than twenty years, whose recuperation I owe to the quality of Sony cassettes that made the reproductions possible. This chapter is adapted from the talk given at the Casa das Rosas.

1 Jorge Luis Borges was named Edward Laroque Tinker Visiting Professor for the 1961 academic year, the poet Cecília Meireles taught a course in the summer of 1946, and Clarice Lispector read a paper on vanguardism at a conference in 1963.

2 Professor Pablo Beltrán de Heredia took the poem and translation to Santander, Spain, where he had a private edition printed of twenty copies in large format, numbered, and eventually signed by the poet and the translator: *VISÃO DO PARAÍSO, Braniff: New York-Austin, 14–IV–78*, with the inscription "translation to English by K. David Jackson. Limited edition of twenty copies, printed by Pablo Beltrán de Heredia, signed by the author and translator, in Taller de Artes Gráficas de Gonzalo Bedia, Santander, Spain, 23 August 1979." This rare publication testifies to the interest of the Spanish faculty in Haroldo's visit and his poetry.

3 Christopher Middleton, "Cabaret de la Canne, January 1855," in *The Word Pavilion and Selected Poems* (Manchester: Carcanet, 2001), 223–226. Note: "Monologue for Gérard de Nerval on the eve of his suicide. Alfred Delvan described such a meeting with him" (323).

4 Christopher Middleton, trans., "Autumn Feeling (1775)," in *Johann Wolfgang von Goethe: Selected Poems*, ed. Christopher Middleton (Boston: Suhrkamp/Insel Publishers, 1983), 42–43.

5 Austin, 1981. Haroldo de Campos, "Logopéia via Goethe via Christopher Middleton," in *O arco-íris branco* (São Paulo: Imago, 1997), 25–26.

Chapter 10 Meeting in Austin

Translated by Tom Winterbottom and Jamille Pinheiro Dias. This remembrance originally appeared in the Revista USP and is reprinted with permission.

1 Excerpt from Haroldo de Campos's poem "Aisthesis Kharis: Iki" in Haroldo de Campos, *A educação dos cinco sentidos* (São Paulo: Brasiliense, 1985), 50.
2 Excerpt from Haroldo de Campos's poem "Aisthesis Kharis: Iki" in Haroldo de Campos, *A educação dos cinco sentidos* (São Paulo: Brasiliense, 1985), 50.

Chapter 11 Three Variations on Octavio Paz's "Blanco" and Fifteen Antiphonals for Haroldo de Campos, with a Note on Translation, Transcreation, and Othering

1 My point of departure for the Blanco variations was Eliot Weinberger's translation of "Blanco" in *The Collected Poems of Octavio Paz* (1991), while Haroldo de Campos's words in *Antiphonals* are drawn from various English translations by A. S. Bessa, Suzanne Jill Levine, Christopher Middleton, Norman Potter, and Charles A. Perrone. My translation from which Lorca Variation XV was constructed can be found in Federico García Lorca, *Collected Poems* (New York: Farrar, Straus and Giroux, 1991, 370–374, along with Lorca's original Spanish.

Chapter 12 Poems

1 Unlike the other poems here, this was published in English. Except for "O país das maravilhas," all poems are from Antonio Cicero's book *Guardar* (Rio de Janeiro: Record, 1996).
2 Translated by Charles A. Perrone.
3 Translated by Arto Lindsay.
4 Translated by Charles A. Perrone.
5 Translated by Charles A. Perrone.
6 Originally published in Antonio Cicero, *A cidade e os livros* (Rio de Janeiro: Record, 2002).
7 Translated by Frederick G. Williams.

Chapter 15 Amberianum (Philosophical Fragments of Caudio Amberian)

1 The translations are Bernstein's.

Bibliography

Auden, W. H. *Another Time*. New York: Random House, 1940.

Baudelaire, Charles. "Le Voyage." In *Œuvres complètes*, edited by Claude Pichois, 122–127. Paris: Gallimard, 1961.

Baudrillard, Jean, "The Art of Disappearance." In *Jean Baudrillard: Art and Artefact*, edited by Nicholas Zurbrugg, 28–31. London: Sage Publications, 1997.

Behnke, Kerstin. "Krise der Repräsentation." In *Historisches Wörterbuch der Philosophie*, edited by Joachim Ritter and Karlfried Gründer, 846–854. Vol. 8. Darmstadt: Wissenschaftliche Buchgesellschaft, 1992.

Blanchot, Maurice. "Où va la littérature?" In *Le livre à venir*, 266–340. Paris: Gallimard, 1959.

Bloch, Ernst. *Das Prinzip Hoffnung*. Frankfurt am Main: Suhrkamp, 1959.

Block de Behar, Lisa, ed. *Haroldo de Campos, don de poesía: Ensayos críticos sobre su obra*. Montevideo: Linardi y Risso, 2009.

Brito, Ronaldo. *Neoconcretismo: Vértice e ruptura do projeto construtivo brasileiro*. Rio de Janeiro: Funarte, 1985.

Brodsky, Joseph, "On 'September 1, 1939' by W. H. Auden." In *Less Than One: Selected Essays*, 304–356. New York: Farrar, Straus and Giroux, 1988.

Campbell, Ewing, and Julio Ortega, eds. *The Plaza of Encounters*. Austin: Latitudes Press, 1981.

Campos, Augusto de. *Poesia da recusa*. São Paulo: Perspectiva, 2006.

Campos, Augusto de, and Haroldo de Campos. *Sousândrade: O terremoto clandestino*. Rio de Janeiro: Instituto Nacional do Livro, 1964.

Campos, Augusto de, Haroldo de Campos, Décio Pignatari, and Stéphane Mallarmé. *Mallarmé*. 2 vols. São Paulo: Editora Perspectiva, Coleção Signos, 1974.

Campos, Haroldo de. *A educação dos cinco sentidos*. São Paulo: Brasiliense, 1985.

———. "A linguagem do Iauaretê." In *Metalinguagem e outras metas: Ensaios de teoria e crítica literária*, 47–53. São Paulo: Perspectiva, 1976.

———. "Da tradução como criação e crítica." In *Metalinguagem e outras metas: Ensaios de teoria e crítica literária*, 31–48. São Paulo: Editora Perspectiva, 1992.

———. *Galáxias*. São Paulo: Editora Ex Libris, 1984. (2nd ed., São Paulo: Editora 34, 2004).

———. *Galaxies*. Preface by Jacques Roubaud. Translated and introduction by Inês Oseki-Dépré and the author. Paris: La Main Courante, 1998.
———. "Hölderlin's Red Word." Translated by Albert Bork. *20th Century Studies* 11 (1974): 4–10.
———. "Logopéia via Goethe via Christopher Middleton." In *O arco-íris branco*, 25–26. São Paulo: Imago, 1997.
———. *Novas: Selected Writings*. Edited by Antonio Sergio Bessa and Odile Cisneros. Evanston, IL: Northwestern University Press, 2007.
———. *O arco-íris branco*. Rio de Janeiro: Imago, 1997.
———. *O sequestro do Barroco na formação da literatura brasileira: O caso Gregório de Matos*. São Paulo: Perspectiva, 1989.
———. "Poesia e modernidade: Da morte da arte à constelação. O poema pós-utópico." In *O arco-íris branco*, 243–269. Rio de Janeiro: Imago, 1997.
Campos, Haroldo de, Antonio Sergio Bessa, and Odile Cisneros. "Anthropophagous Reason: Dialogue and Difference in Brazilian Culture." In *Novas: Selected Writings*, edited by Antonio Sergio Bessa and Odile Cisneros, 157–177. Evanston, IL: Northwestern University Press, 2007.
———. "Translation as Creation and Criticism." In *Novas: Selected Writings*, edited by Antonio Sergio Bessa and Odile Cisneros, 312–326. Evanston, IL: Northwestern University Press, 2007.
Cantú, Roberto, ed. *The Willow and the Spiral: Essays on Octavio Paz and the Poetic Imagination*. Newcastle: Cambridge Scholars Publishing, 2014.
Carpenter, Victoria. "From Yellow to Red to Black: Tantric Reading of 'Blanco' by Octavio Paz." *Bulletin of Latin American Research* 21, no. 4 (2002): 527–544.
Carvalhal, Tania Franco. "La tradition du Haikú dans la poésie Latine-Américaine: Un cas de médiation." In *ICLA '91 Tokyo: The Force of Vision, II: Visions in History; Visions of the Other*, edited by Earl Miner, et al., 383–390. Tokyo: Internat. Compar. Lit. Assn, 1995.
Cicero, Antonio. *A cidade e os livros*. Rio de Janeiro: Record, 2002.
———. *Guardar*. Rio de Janeiro: Record, 1996.
———. *O mundo desde o fim*. São Paulo: Companhia das Letras, 2005.
———. "Poesia e paisagens urbanas." In *Finalidades sem fim*, 14–30. São Paulo: Companhia das Letras, 2005.
Cisneros, Odile. "Isomorphism to Cannibalism: The Evolution of Haroldo de Campos's Translation Concepts." *Traduction, Terminologie, Rédaction* 25, no. 2 (2012): 15–44.
cummings, ee, and Augusto de Campos. *40 Poem(a)s*. 2nd ed. São Paulo: Brasiliense, 1986.
Daintith, John. "Isomorphism." In *Dictionary of Chemistry*. 6th ed. Oxford: Oxford University Press, 2008. DOI: 10.1093/acref/9780199204632.001.000.
Dasgupta, Shashibhusan. *An Introduction to Tantric Buddhism*. Calcutta: University of Calcutta, 1958.
Dasilva, Xosé Manuel. "Octavio Paz transcreado por Haroldo de Campos: De *Blanco* a *Transblanco*." *Trans* 10 (2006): 23–40.
Derrida, Jacques. *La dissémination*. Paris: Seuil, 1972.
Drummond de Andrade, Carlos. *Claro enigma*. São Paulo: Companhia das Letras, 2012.
Fein, John M. *Toward Octavio Paz: A Reading of His Major Poems 1957–1976*. Lexington: University Press of Kentucky, 1986.
Foucault, Michel. *Les mots et les choses*. Paris: Gallimard, 1966.

Gell, Alfred. *Art and Agency: An Anthropological Theory*. Oxford: Clarendon, 1998.

Gimferrer, Pere. *Lecturas de Octavio Paz*. Barcelona: Anagrama, 1980.

Gruesz, Kirsten Silva. *Ambassadors of Culture: The Transamerican Origins of Latino Writing*. Princeton, NJ: Princeton University Press, 2001.

Infante, Ignacio. *After Translation: The Transfer and Circulation of Modern Poetics across the Atlantic*. New York: Fordham University Press, 2013.

Iser, Wolfgang. *Das Fiktive und das Imaginäre: Perspektiven literarischer Anthropologie*. Frankfurt am Main: Suhrkamp, 1991.

———. *The Fictive and the Imaginary: Charting Literary Anthropology*. Baltimore: Johns Hopkins University Press, 1993.

Jackson, K. David, and Albert Bork, trans. *Seraphim Grosse Pointe*. Austin: Nefertiti Head Press, 1979.

Jameson, Frederic. "Imaginary and Symbolic in Lacan." In *The Ideologies of Theory: Essays 1971–1986*, 77–124. London: Routledge, 1988.

Kant, Immanuel. *Kritik der reinen Vernunft*. Frankfurt am Main: Suhrkamp, 1976.

Kopenawa, Davi, and Bruce Albert. *A queda do céu: Palavras de um xamã yanomami*. Translated by Beatriz Perrone-Moisés. São Paulo: Companhia das Letras, 2010.

Lafer, Celso, Haroldo de Campos, and Andrés Sánchez Robayna. "Conversación Sobre Octavio Paz." *Cuadernos Hispanoamericanos: Revista Mensual de Cultura Hispánica* 558 (1996): 7–27.

Latour, Bruno. *We Have Never Been Modern*. Translated by Catherine Porter. Cambridge, MA: Harvard University Press, 1993.

Lorca, Federico García. *Collected Poems*. New York: Farrar, Straus and Giroux, 1991.

Lyotard, Jean-François. *The Lyotard Reader*. Edited by Andrew Benjamin. Oxford: Basil Blackwell, 1989.

Machado, Antonio. *Poesias de Guerra (1936–1939). Border of a Dream. Selected Poems*. Bilingual ed. Translated and introduction by Willis Barnstone. Port Townsend, WA: Copper Canyon Press, 2004.

Maciel, Maria Esther. "América Latina reinventada: Octavio Paz e Haroldo De Campos." *Revista Iberoamericana* 64, nos.182–183 (1998): 219–228.

Mallarmé, Stéphane. *Collected Poems*. Bilingual ed. Translated and with a commentary by Henry Weinfield. Berkeley: University of California Press, 1994.

———. *Divigations*. Paris: Bibliothéque-Charpentier, 1897.

———. "Observation relative au poème 'Un coup de dés jamais n'abolira le Hasard.'" In *Œuvres complètes*, edited by Bertrand Marchal, 391–392. Paris: Gallimard, 1998.

———. *Œuvres complètes*. Edited by Bertrand Marchal. Paris: Gallimard, 1998.

Malpartida, Juan. "Octavio Paz el traductor (Analogía y crítica)." *Revista de Occidente* 403 (2014): 36–61.

McGuirk, Bernard, and Else R. P. Vieira, eds. *Haroldo de Campos: In Conversation*. London: Zoilus Press, 2009.

Middleton, Christopher, trans. "Autumn Feeling (1775)." In *Johann Wolfgang von Goethe: Selected Poems*, ed. Christopher Middleton, 42–43. Boston: Suhrkamp/Insel Publishers, 1983.

———. "Cabaret de la Canne, January 1855." In *The Word Pavilion and Selected Poems*, 223–226. Manchester: Carcanet, 2001.

Middleton, Christopher, and Norman Potter, trans. "passtimes & killtimes." *Via* 1 (May 1976): 55–57.

Milán, Eduardo. "Tensão do dizer em *Blanco* de Octavio Paz." In Octavio Paz and Haroldo de Campos, *Transblanco*, 159–171. São Paulo: Editora Siciliano, 1986.

Nóbrega, Manuel da. "Carta (1549)." In *Cartas dos primeiros jesuitas no Brasil*, edited by Serafim Leite. Vol 1. Lisbon: Livraria Portugalia, 1956.
Norbu, Namkhai. *Dzogchen: The Self-Perfected State*. Translated by John Shane. New York: Snow Lion, 1989.
Ortega, Julio. "*Blanco:* Space of Change." *World Literature Today* 56, no. 4 (Autumn 1982): 635–638.
———. "Concrete Poetry and Beyond: A Conversation between Julio Ortega and Haroldo de Campos." *Review: Literature and Arts of the Americas* 19, no. 36 (1986): 36–45.
Paz, Octavio. *Alternating Current*. New York: Viking Press, 1973.
———. *Árbol adentro*. Barcelona: Seix Barral, 1987.
———. *Blanco*. Mexico, D.F.: Ediciones del Equilibrista, 1995.
———. *The Bow and the Lyre: The Poem. The Poetic Revelation. Poetry and History*. Translated by Ruth L. C. Simms. Austin: University of Texas Press, 1973.
———. *Claude Lévi-Strauss: An Introduction*. Translated by J. S. Bernstein. Ithaca, NY: Cornell University Press, 1970.
———. *The Collected Poems of Octavio Paz: 1957–1987*. Edited by Eliot Weinberger. New York: New Directions, 1991.
———. *Configurations*. With an introduction by Muriel Rukeyser. New York: New Directions, 1971.
———. *Convergences*. Translated by Helen Lane. New York: Harcourt Brace, 1987.
———. *El arco y la lira*. 2nd ed., rev. Mexico City: Fondo de Cultura Económica, 1967.
———. *El mono gramático*. Barcelona: Seix Barral, 1974.
———. *Excursiones/incursiones: Dominio extranjero*. 2nd ed. Barcelona: Círculo de Lectores, 1994.
———. *Ladera este (1962–1968)*. Mexico DF: Joaquín Mortiz, 1969.
———. *La otra voz: Poesía y fin de siglo*. Barcelona: Seix Barral, 1990.
———. *L'Arc et la lyre*. Translated by Roger Munier. Paris: Gallimard, 1965.
———. *Le singe grammairien*. Translated by Claude Esteban. Geneva: A. Skira, 1972.
———. "The Literal and the Literary." *TLS: The Times Literary Supplement*, September 18, 1970, 1019–1021.
———. *The Monkey Grammarian*. Translated by Helen R. Lane. New York: Seaver Books-Grove Press, 1981.
———. Octavio Paz to Haroldo de Campos, March 14, 1968. In Octavio Paz and Haroldo de Campos, *Transblanco*, 98–103. São Paulo: Editora Siciliano, 1986.
———. "¿Poesía latinoamericana?" In *El signo y el garabato*, 175–189. Barcelona: Seix Barral, 1991.
———. "Poetry and Modernity." Translated by Eliot Weinberger. In *The Tanner Lectures on Human Values*. Delivered at the University of Utah, October 18–20, 1989. http://tannerlectures.utah.edu/_documents/a-to-z/p/Paz98.pdf.
———. *Tiempo nublado*. Barcelona: Seix Barral, 1983.
———. "Traducción: Literatura y literalidad." In *Traducción: Literatura y literalidad*, 7–19. Barcelona: Tusquets Editor, 1971.
———. "The Word as Foundation." *Times Literary Supplement*, November 14, 1968, 1283–1284.
Paz, Octavio, and Haroldo de Campos. *Transblanco: Em torno a* Blanco *de Octavio Paz*. São Paulo: Editora Siciliano, 1986.
———. *Transblanco: Em torno a* Blanco *de Octavio Paz*. 2nd ed. São Paulo: Editora Siciliano, 1994.

Paz, Octavio, and Nicanor Vélez. *Versiones y diversiones*. Bilingual ed. Barcelona: Galaxia Gutenberg, Círculo de Lectores, 2000.

Perloff, Marjorie. "From Avant-Garde to Digital: The Legacy of Brazilian Concrete Poetry." In *Unoriginal Genius: Poetry by Other Means in the New Century*, 50–75. Chicago: University of Chicago Press, 2010.

Perrone, Charles A. "De Gregório de Matos a Caetano Veloso e 'Outras palavras': Barroquismo na Música Popular Brasileira contemporânea." *Revista Iberoamericana* 50, no.126 (1984): 77–99.

———. "4 × 3 × 2 = Quadrangulating Triangular Pairs: Simultaneous Versions of a Vital Concrete Poem." *Tradução em revista* 6 (2009): 1–17.

———. "Notas para facilitar a leitura de 'Meu tio o iauaretê.'" *Hispania* 91, no. 4 (2008): 766–774.

Pessoa, Fernando. "Opiário." In *Ficções do interlúdio*, edited by Fernando Cabral Martins, 105–112. Lisbon: Assírio & Alvim, 1998.

Pound, Ezra. *ABC of Reading*. New York: New Directions, 2010.

———. "Canto 77." In *The Cantos*, 466. New York: New Directions, 1970.

Quiroga, José. *Understanding Octavio Paz*. Columbia: University of South Carolina Press, 1999.

Rimbaud, Arthur. "Mouvement." In *L'oeuvre*, 409. Paris: Textuel, 2000.

Ritter, Joachim, and Karlfried Gründer, eds. *Historisches Wörterbuch der Philosophie*. Vol. 8. Darmstadt: Wissenschaftliche Buchgesellschaft, 1992.

Rodríguez García, José María. "John Donne after Octavio Paz: Translation as Transculturation." *Dispositio/n: American Journal of Cultural Histories and Theories* 48 (1999): 155–182.

———. "Literary into Cultural Translation." In "Literature into Cultural Translation," edited by J. M. Rodríguez García. Special issue, *diacritics* 34, nos. 3–4 (Fall-Winter 2004): 3–30.

Rodríguez Monegal, Emir. "Blanco/Branco: Transblanco." In Octavio Paz and Haroldo de Campos, *Transblanco*, 13–19. São Paulo: Editora Siciliano, 1994.

Román-Odio, Clara. "'Blanco', a Western Mandala." *Revista Canadiense de Estudios Hispánicos* 24, no. 3 (2000): 503–515.

Sandoval, Rodolfo Mata. "Haroldo de Campos y Octavio Paz: Del diálogo creativo a la mediación institucional en América Latina." *Latinoamérica* 30 (2001): 131–154.

———. "Transblanco de Octavio Paz y Haroldo de Campos." *Vuelta* 216 (1994): 2.

Santí, Enrico Mario. *El acto de las palabras: Estudios y diálogos con Octavio Paz*. Mexico City: Fondo de Cultura Económica, 1997.

———. *El acto de las palabras: Estudios y diálogos con Octavio Paz*. Rev. ed. Mexico City: Fondo de Cultura Económica, 2015.

———. "Esto no es un poema." In *Blanco/Archivo Blanco*, edited by Enrico Mario Santí, 235–321. Mexico City: Ediciones del Equilibrista, 1995.

Solt, Mary Ellen. *Concrete Poetry: A World View*. Bloomington: Indiana University Press, 1970.

Tenório da Motta, Leda, ed. *Céu acima: Para um "tombeau" de Haroldo de Campos*. São Paulo: Perspectiva, 2005.

Tesauro, Emanuele. "Arguzie umane." In *Il cannocchiale Aristotelico o sia Idea dell'arguta et ingeniosa elocutione che serve à tutta l' arte oratoria, lapidaria; et simbolica esaminata co' principii del divino Aristotele*, 82–107. 5th ed. Turin: Zavatta, 1670.

Ulacia, Manuel. "El árbol milenario: Octavio Paz y Haroldo De Campos." *Siglo XX/20th Century* 10, nos. 1–2 (1992): 221–229.

———. *El árbol milenario: Un recorrido por la obra de Octavio Paz.* Barcelona: Galaxia Gutenberg, 1999.

Weinberger, Eliot. "Paz in Asia." In *Outside Stories*, 17–45. New York: New Directions, 1992.

Wilson, Jason. *Octavio Paz: A Study of His Poetics*. Cambridge: Cambridge University Press, 1979.

Notes on Contributors

CHARLES BERNSTEIN is the author of the essay collection *Pitch of Poetry* (2016), which includes a piece on Haroldo de Campos, and the poetry collections *Near/Miss* (2018) and *Recalculating* (2013). Bernstein is Donald T. Regan Professor of English and Comparative Literature at the University of Pennsylvania, where he is co-director of PennSound.

ANTONIO CICERO is a Brazilian composer, poet, and philosopher. He has worked with Marina Lima, Waly Salomão, João Bosco, Adriana Calcanhotto, José Miguel Wisnik, and many others. He is the author of the philosophy books *O mundo desde o fim* (1995), *Finalidades sem fim* (2005), *Poesia e filosofia* (2012), and *A poesia e a crítica* (2017), and the author of the poetry books *Guardar* (1996), *A cidade e os livros* (2002), *O Livro de sombras* (2011), and *Porventura* (2012). He is also the editor of *Forma e sentido contemporâneo* (2012) and the co-editor of *O relativismo enquanto visão do mundo* (1994), with Waly Salomão, and of *Nova antologia poética de Vinícius de Moraes* (2003), with Eucanaã Ferraz. In 2012, he was awarded the Prêmio Alceu Amoroso Lima—Poesia e Liberdade. In 2017 he was elected a member of the Brazilian Academy of Letters. He is currently a member of the directory of União Brasileira de Compositores.

ODILE CISNEROS earned a PhD from New York University and currently teaches in the Department of Modern Languages and Cultural Studies at the University of Alberta in Edmonton, Alberta, Canada. With Richard Young she coauthored *Historical Dictionary of Latin American Literature* (2011). She also co-edited *Novas: Selected Writings* of Haroldo de Campos with A. S. Bessa (2007). She has authored a complete translation of Haroldo de Campos's poetic prose *Galáxias*, partly available at http://www.artsrn.ualberta.ca/galaxias/. Professor Cisneros specializes in the Latin American historical avant-gardes, modern and contemporary Brazilian poetry, Mexican literature, literary translation, and environmental approaches to literature.

JOÃO ADOLFO HANSEN is professor emeritus of Brazilian literature at the Universidade de São Paulo. He researches Luso-Brazilian practices of representation in the seventeenth and eighteenth centuries. Among his books are *A sátira e o engenho: Gregório de Matos e a Bahia do século XVII* (1989), *Carlos Bracher* (1997), and *OO. A ficção da literatura em Grande Sertão: Veredas* (2000). He has published several articles in specialized journals. He received the Prêmio Jabuti in 1990 in the book essay category and the 2014 Grand Prize of the São Paulo Association of Art Critics. His work centers on literature with an emphasis on comparative studies of Lusophone literatures.

KENNETH DAVID JACKSON is professor of Portuguese at Yale University. He specializes in Portuguese and Brazilian literatures, modernist movements in literature and other arts, Portuguese literature and culture in Asia, poetry, music, and ethnography. His books include *Machado de Assis: A Literary Life* (2015) and *Adverse Genres in Fernando Pessoa* (2010). He is editor of the *Oxford Anthology of the Brazilian Short Story* (2006) and *Haroldo de Campos: A Dialogue with the Brazilian Concrete Poet* (2005).

MARÍLIA LIBRANDI is visiting assistant professor of Brazilian studies at Princeton University. She had taught at Universidade Estadual do Sudoeste da Bahia before moving to Stanford University, where she taught in the Department of Iberian and Latin American Cultures from 2009 to 2018. Her research focuses on the study of the novel and modern poetry, Indigenous thought, and literary theory. She is the author of *Writing by Ear: Clarice Lispector and the Aural Novel* (2018) and of *Maranhão-Manhattan: Ensaios de Literatura Brasileira* (2009). She is co-director of the research group *Estudos da Escuta* (Cnpq/Brazil) and affiliated faculty of Diversitas (Núcleo de Estudos das Diversidades, Intolerâncias e Conflitos) at the Universidade de São Paulo.

LUIZ COSTA LIMA is professor emeritus at Pontifícia Universadade Católica do Rio de Janeiro. In 2004, he received the foreign researcher of the year award from the Alexander von Humboldt Foundation (Germany) in the humanities. In 2011, the University of Queensland (Australia) hosted the international colloquium "Mimesis and Culture," dedicated to his work. He has written more than twenty books, including *Mimesis: desafio ao pensamento* (2000) and *O controle do imaginário e a afirmação do romance* (2009), which was awarded prizes from the Academia Brasileira de Letras and the Biblioteca Nacional.

BENEDITO NUNES (1929–2011) was a professor, art critic, philosopher, and writer and was widely recognized as among the most important voices in Brazilian cultural criticism. He taught in Brazil, France, and the United States. He won the Prêmio Jabuti in 1987 and again in 2010, the same year he was awarded Prêmio Machado de Assis by the Academia Brasileira de Letras for his life's work.

MARJORIE PERLOFF, until her retirement from Stanford in 2003, held the Sadie D. Patek Chair of Humanities in the English Department. She is also Florence Scott Professor Emerita at the University of Southern California. Among her many books on modernist and postmodernist poetics and visual arts are *The Futurist Moment: Avant-Garde, Avant-Guerre and the Language of Rupture*, *Wittgenstein's Ladder*, *Unoriginal Genius: Poetry by Other Means in the New Century*, and, most recently, *Edge of Irony: Modernism in the Shadow of the Habsburg Empire*. She gave the keynote lecture at a celebration of Augusto de Campos's poetry and art work in São Paulo in July 2016.

CHARLES A. PERRONE is professor emeritus of Portuguese and Luso-Brazilian culture and literature in the Department of Spanish and Portuguese Studies at the University of Florida. He is the author of *Masters of Contemporary Brazilian Song: MPB 1965–1985* (1989), *Seven Faces: Brazilian Poetry since Modernism* (1996), and *Brazil, Lyric, and the Americas* (2010). He is co-editor of *Crônicas brasileiras: A Reader* and *Brazilian Popular Music and Globalization*. In addition to many articles and book chapters on Brazilian literature and popular music, he has translated numerous contemporary Brazilian writers, most notably poets Augusto de Campos and Paulo Leminski.

JAMILLE PINHEIRO DIAS is a postdoctoral fellow in translation studies at the Department of Modern Languages at the University of São Paulo and holds a PhD in English from the same institution. She was a visiting researcher in Iberian and Latin American cultures at Stanford University, and a teaching assistant at the Institute of Brazilian Studies at the University of São Paulo. Her research interests involve translation studies, Indigenous peoples, human rights, and activism.

JEROME ROTHENBERG is an internationally celebrated poet with over ninety books of poetry and twelve assemblages of traditional and avant-garde poetry, including *Technicians of the Sacred* and *Poems for the Millennium*, volumes 1–3. Recent books of poems include *Retrievals: Uncollected & New Poems 1955–2010*, *A Field on Mars: Poems 2000–2015*, and *The President of Desolation*. His most recent big books are *Eye of Witness: A Jerome Rothenberg Reader* and *Barbaric Vast & Wild: Outside & Subterranean Poetry from Origins to Present*. He is currently working on a transnational anthology of North and South American poetry from pre-Columbian times to the present.

ENRICO MARIO SANTÍ is research professor at Claremont Graduate University, Claremont, California, and William T. Bryan Endowed Chair in Hispanic Studies at the University of Kentucky, Lexington. He is a specialist in Latin American and comparative literature. With degrees from Vanderbilt and Yale, he has taught at Duke, Cornell, and Georgetown and was the youngest holder of the Bacardí Chair in Cuban Studies at the University of Miami. Awarded Guggenheim, Wilson, Fulbright-Hays, ACLS, and NEH fellowships, he has been visiting professor at UC Riverside, Claremont McKenna College, Claremont Graduate University, and Chile's Universidad Católica. Santí is the author of ten books, including the landmark *El acto de las palabras: Estudios y diálogos con Octavio Paz* (1998; revised edition, 2016); twenty edited volumes, among which is the stunning *Blanco/Archivo Blanco* (1998); and has lectured widely in the United States, Latin America, Europe, and Asia. Among Santí's current projects are an intellectual biography of Octavio Paz and translations of the work of Cuban American poet Ricardo Pau-Llosa.

KEIJIRO SUGA is a Tokyo-based poet and critic. He has published ten books of critical essays, of which *Transversal Journeys* (2010) was awarded the Yomiuri Prize for Literature in 2011. *Agend'Ars* is a series of sixteen-line poems consisting of 256 pieces. These were published in four separate volumes from 2010 to 2013, and a selected Spanish translation appeared in Mexico in 2015. His fifth book of poetry, *Numbers and Twilight*, was published in 2017. His first poetry book in English, *Transit Blues*, was published by the University of Canberra in 2018, followed by a Spanish translation (2019). He is a prolific translator, and his translations from French, Spanish, and English into Japanese include works by such authors as Edouard Glissant, J. M. G. Le Clézio, Maryse Condé, Isabel Allende, Jamaica Kincaid, and Aimee Bender. He teaches critical theory at Meiji University, Tokyo.

ANDRÉ VALLIAS is a poet and graphic designer. He has published poems and translations in several Brazilian and international magazines, and curated major exhibitions of visual and digital poetry. In 2011 he released *Heine, hein?*, the most comprehensive anthology of the work of Heinrich Heine in Portuguese. In 2014 he published the book-album *Totem*, with an introduction by anthropologist Eduardo Viveiros de Castro, and in 2015 he published *Oratorio*, with an afterword by Alexandre Nodari.

TOM WINTERBOTTOM holds a PhD in Iberian and Latin American cultures. He teaches Latin American literature, culture, and language at Stanford University. His first book, *A Cultural History of Rio de Janeiro after 1889: Glorious Decadence*, came out in 2016.

Index